PRAISE FOR *INDELIBLE LEADERSHIP* BY MICHAEL FULLAN

"The reach of Michael Fullan's ideas has no limits. He sets out how leaders can forge a path of lasting improvement. As usual, he identifies a critical issue that we should have known—every leader leaves at some point, and if too much depends on a leader, the chances for continuity are seriously compromised. Learn how to make a deep impact today in a way that leaves a growing legacy for tomorrow."

Avis Glaze
Educ-Quest International

"Few today have broader and deeper insights than Michael Fullan in helping to develop leadership amidst the crosscurrents of today's school environments. That students themselves are the hidden agents for deep change, and that the real leadership capabilities needed today can be learned, are just two of Fullan's timely insights in *Indelible Leadership*."

Peter Senge
MIT and Academy for Systemic Change

"This book provides a wonderfully clear and concise guide for education leaders who want to make a real difference in the midst of challenging times. Fullan is a master!"

Tony Wagner, Author
The Global Achievement Gap and *Creating Innovators*

(Continued)

(Continued)

"Indelible Leadership challenges and guides leaders to help students and teachers learn deeply. Fullan has shown why new leadership is crucial for our time, and, more significantly, he reveals what it looks like in practice. Read it and take your leadership to a deeper level!"

Laura Schwalm, Senior Partner
California Education Partners

"Indelible Leadership is quite simply fantastic! Fullan's book offers an exceptional framework for action in our complex times. It provides tools, lots of gems and surprising insights, and thought-provoking challenges. I found myself immediately putting these ideas into practice. As a long-time consultant on transformational leadership, Fullan has already 'left this reader learning.'"

Mike East, General Manager, K–12 Education
IBM Canada Ltd.

Indelible
Leadership

Corwin Impact Leadership Series

Series Editor: Peter M. DeWitt

Principal Voice: Listen, Learn, Lead by Russell J. Quaglia

Indelible Leadership: Always Leave Them Learning by Michael Fullan

Teaching for Greatness: Learner-Driven Education by Yong Zhao

And forthcoming contributions from

- Avis Glaze
- Andy Hargreaves
- Viviane Robinson
- Pasi Sahlberg

Indelible Leadership

Always Leave Them Learning

Michael Fullan

Corwin Impact Leadership Series

Series Editor: Peter M. DeWitt

A Joint Publication

ONTARIO PRINCIPALS' COUNCIL
Exemplary Leadership in Public Education

For information:

Corwin
A SAGE Company
2455 Teller Road
Thousand Oaks, California 91320
(800) 233-9936
www.corwin.com

SAGE Publications Ltd.
1 Oliver's Yard
55 City Road
London EC1Y 1SP
United Kingdom

SAGE Publications India Pvt. Ltd.
B 1/I 1 Mohan Cooperative Industrial Area
Mathura Road, New Delhi 110 044
India

SAGE Publications Asia-Pacific Pte. Ltd.
3 Church Street
#10-04 Samsung Hub
Singapore 049483

Printed in the United States of America

Library of Congress Cataloging-in-Publication Data

Names: Fullan, Michael, author.

Title: Indelible leadership : always leave them learning / Michael Fullan.

Description: Thousand Oaks, California : Corwin, a SAGE Company, 2016. | Series: Corwin impact leadership series | Includes bibliographical references and index.

Identifiers: LCCN 2016011379 | ISBN 9781506323626 (pbk. : alk. paper)

Subjects: LCSH: Leadership.

Classification: LCC HD57.7 .F853 2016 | DDC 658.4/092—dc23
LC record available at https://lccn.loc.gov/2016011379

This book is printed on acid-free paper.

Executive Editor: Arnis Burvikovs
Senior Associate Editor: Desirée A. Bartlett
Senior Editorial Assistant: Andrew Olson
Production Editor: Melanie Birdsall
Copy Editor: Diana Breti
Typesetter: C&M Digitals (P) Ltd.
Proofreader: Caryne Brown
Indexer: Molly Hall
Cover Designer: Michael Dubowe
Marketing Manager: Anna Mesick

Certified Chain of Custody
SUSTAINABLE FORESTRY INITIATIVE
Promoting Sustainable Forestry
www.sfiprogram.org
SFI-01268

SFI label applies to text stock

16 17 18 19 20 10 9 8 7 6 5 4 3 2 1

Contents

To the wisdom of human evolution

Preface

Leaders and would-be leaders today face double jeopardy. The demands on them are multifarious, disjointed, relentless, and chaotic. And the advice they receive—from their bosses, books, workshops, job descriptions, and consultants—is an amalgam of half-truths, vague generalities, piecemeal solutions, and ad hoc good ideas. Yet there has never been a time when the contribution of good leaders is more urgently required. *Indelible leadership* is a term I use interchangeably with *deep leadership*: Leaders who self-consciously focus on deep change and do so by mobilizing other leaders at all levels of the system, thereby building capacity for today and for tomorrow. If such leaders learn every day and help others learn how to learn, they know that when it comes time to depart they can always leave them learning. We need deep leadership devoted to achieving deep learning outcomes.

The deep learning outcomes are what we now call the *global competencies* or the 6Cs: *character, citizenship, collaboration, communication, creativity,* and *critical thinking*. The question I pursue in this book is what kind of leadership qualities will produce such learning outcomes for the whole system. (Let's not quibble over the global competencies at this point; my leadership qualities will be valuable for any deep learning outcomes).

My goal is to distill leadership knowledge and skills into a set of attributes that is graspable, manageable, mutually reinforcing, and synergistic in its impact. The domains of leadership that I identify can be learned and can be fostered in others with whom our indelible leaders work. Indelible, of course, means lasting, permanent, impossible to forget or to eradicate. To do this you have to go deep—very deep—and you have to take a lot of people with you (and sometimes, as we shall see, you have to let people take you deep). You have to always be innovating and consolidating—the twin sinews of fluid permanency.

For this to be possible you need to master a small number of attributes that you can concentrate on and that reinforce one another through use. As you do this, the ideas and practices become increasingly embedded in the collectivity. There is a confluence of forces that is currently conspiring to generate conditions favorable to the deep change agenda. Maintaining the status quo is impossible, partly because of the dramatic changes in the world at large but also because traditional schooling is no longer relevant or engaging. These forces call for leaders who stimulate and are responsive to youth's tendency for breakaway behavior when it comes to passionate learning and its link to the possibility of more interesting and productive lives, especially concerning the natural human tendency to do something worthwhile for oneself and for humanity.

Helping humanity is a natural evolutionary instinct. It fails to appear in some individuals and under some conditions, but it always ends up on top over time. One of the main reasons for this inevitability is that education favors the humanity theme. Thus leaders can do all of us a favor by uncovering and unleashing our individual and social potential for helping ourselves as we help humanity. Deep leadership makes this happen for today, for tomorrow, and in an evolutionary sense, forever.

I am not claiming that all the innovative educational ideas in this book are brand-new, but what is new is that they are happening in everyday schools on an increasing scale, especially the emerging phenomenon of students as radical change agents. What is new are some key leadership insights about how to lead this deep change transformation.

The leadership model can be seen as a set of six tensions that must be managed. How can leaders (1) combine moral imperative and uplifting leadership, (2) master content and process, (3) lead and learn in equal measure, (4) see students as change agents, (5) feed and be fed by the system, and (6) be essential and dispensable? This book is about managing these six difficult tensions. Subsequent chapters will tell you how to lead in this dynamic world.

Author's Note

Deep Leadership:
Managing Six Big Tensions

I t is significant that the concept of *depth* is rapidly coming to the fore when we talk of so many things that matter, such as beliefs, relationships, learning, and the meaning of life itself. Paradoxically, the recent focus on depth may be because the world is awash with superficiality. Humans can stand only so much triviality before our evolutionary instincts kick in and people become receptive to the question "What are we here for?" What, indeed, is the purpose of life, of work, of being? At first the idea that something might be wrong, even radically wrong, can lie dormant. People keep on doing what they have been doing until something or someone disturbs the status quo and reveals fundamental flaws that cannot be ignored. This is what deep leaders do. They help unleash, uncover, ferret out, extract, and enable new ways of thinking and acting.

Revealingly, flaws are rarely the starting point for deep leaders. They can be just as surprised as anyone at what turns up once they help create certain change dynamics focused on high-leverage questions and processes. Indelible leaders have a knack for uncovering and helping the group pursue new ideas that solve problems in ways never before experienced. It involves complex and hard work that does not seem unreasonable for those doing it—because they become individually and collectively motivated to keep on going deeper. People become so immersed that what they are doing doesn't even seem like work.

We see this phenomenon in our global leadership initiative New Pedagogies for Deep Learning, or "Deep Learning" for short (www .npdl.global). The negative impetus (that makes some action inevitable) is that traditional schooling is boring as you go up the grade levels. By the time students reach Grade 9 or 10, only a little over one-third are engaged. And needless to say, teachers are not all that happy (teaching the bored is at least one step more unsettling than being bored). To be clear, there are some fantastically interesting teachers, classes, and schools, but they are in the minority, and the current culture and structure will always contain their spread. Indelible leadership concerns *systemic change*—practical, realistic, probable change across the whole system.

> Indelible leaders have a knack for uncovering and helping the group pursue new ideas that solve problems in ways never before experienced.

Our motto in Deep Learning—our value proposition—is "Helping humanity change the world." In keeping with my main argument, I should stress that this propensity to help humanity, as part of helping ourselves be human, is a natural force in our evolutionary makeup.

> Our motto in Deep Learning—our value proposition—is "Helping humanity change the world."

Currently in our Deep Learning initiative we have more than 700 schools (and growing) in networks and clusters in seven countries (Australia, Canada, Finland, Netherlands, New Zealand, United States, and Uruguay) that have readily joined to create alternatives to the present system. I have already mentioned the deep learning outcomes as the 6Cs or global competencies.

The 6Cs

1. Character
2. Citizenship
3. Collaboration
4. Communication
5. Creativity
6. Critical thinking

The Deep Learning pedagogies consist of learning partnerships between and among students, teachers, and families in the pursuit of deep learning experiences and outcomes. Together we are co-creating powerful breakthroughs and insights, such as how readily children can be activated to take control of and responsibility for their own learning, how naturally they take to actions that are focused on "helping humanity," and, indeed, how suited they are to becoming change agents (10-year-olds, for example, are great forces for societal change; for a snippet, see Fullan, 2015c). Deep Learning and its corresponding leadership from many quarters permeate this work. In later chapters, I will provide several concrete examples of the nature of these changes and the kind of leadership that stimulates and responds to these developments.

Cal Newport, a computer scientist, social critic, and consultant based at Georgetown University, has a new book. Guess what it is called? *Deep Work: Rules for Focused Success in a Distracted World* (2016). We will return to this book later when we examine solutions to superficiality. Kaufmann and Gregoire (2015) say that people are "wired to create," but something goes wrong with the wiring as we experience a counter-creative world, including schooling. The business professor and neuroscientist Alan Watkins (2014) shows how most leadership focuses on the tip of the iceberg (results and behavior) whereas the depth is found in thinking, feeling, emotion, and even physiology (physical and mental well-being). My colleague Andy Hargreaves and his team delve into *Uplifting Leadership* in especially high-performing organizations and uncover many of the dimensions of what I have called "indelible leadership" (Hargreaves, Boyle, & Harris, 2014). We will take up these and other ideas in the following chapters.

The above set of "depth probers" address many of the same overlapping issues (and this is the good news), such as passion, meaning, collaboration, solitude, coherence, imagination, creativity, overcoming adversity, high performance, sustainable success, and so on. But alas (and this is the troubling news), most people find these concepts overwhelming and anything but straightforward. My goal in this short book, then, is to portray this new knowledge in a way that is accessible. I have tried to capture just the right amount of complexity that is essential for going deep and is achievable for anyone willing to go for it. I warn the reader that it is hard (especially at the beginning) to become as good as you will need to be, so expect to invest time and persist. The payoff, however, will come sooner than later, and it will come through surges of energy and periodic breakthroughs. I can also pretty much guarantee, as I said above, that it won't seem like hard work once you and others are immersed in it because the focused energy that is generated is irresistible. The forces you generate are beyond your direct control but not beyond your influence.

As noted earlier, I have boiled down the main themes to six interlocking tensions (see Figure 1).

1. Breakthrough moral imperative and uplifting leadership

2. Master content and process

3. Lead and learn in equal measure

4. See students as change agents and protégés

5. Feed and be fed by the system

6. Be essential and dispensable

I will introduce them briefly in this Author's Note so that the reader gets a quick overview. I will then devote a chapter to each of the six. The first tension to manage involves how to combine "moral imperative" and "ubiquitous uplifting leadership." Moral imperative is about one's commitment to what we do. We can use several synonyms for this attribute: identity, passion, and meaning. We will see that establishing a strong identity with a cause is tricky in that you can't just *will* moral imperative in yourself or *demand it* in others. You certainly can't get it directly. (How do you get passion, anyway? And is it possible to have "too much passion"? The answer is yes.) Crucially, because we are talking about deep change in a superficial situation, you are going to have to break through the status quo without knowing exactly how things

Figure 1   Deep Leadership: Six Big Tensions

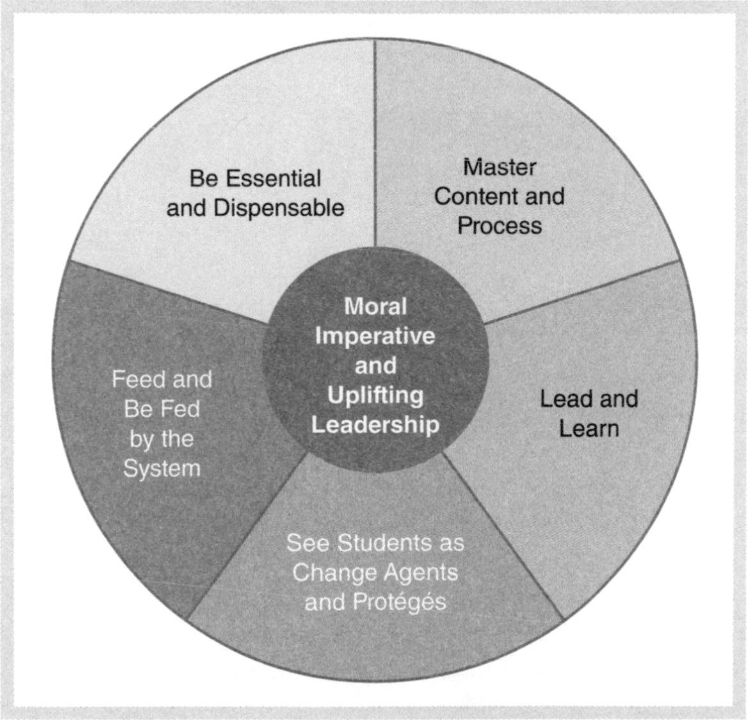

will turn out. In order to do this you will need to mobilize moral imperative through what Andy Hargreaves and his team (2014) have called a spirit of "uplifting leadership" that inspires emotional and spiritual engagement in relation to improved performance.

Fortunately, if you address all six tensions you will garner many allies and many good answers to the "What to do?" dilemmas. You will need leadership in every quarter to move the system, but how do you achieve that and retain coherence? The complex answer right now is that you have to name and focus on "breakthrough moral imperative" and "ubiquitous leadership" and make the combination come alive through the other five dimensions. In this sense, none of the six sets of tensions are stepwise. All six are pursued simultaneously.

The second big leadership quality concerns managing the tension of the relationship between the *content* of a given change and the *process*. By that I mean on the one hand, the content of a given change idea should get shaped and reshaped as people grapple with its best implementation, and, on the other hand, leaders must adapt the process of change to how people are responding and the issues they raise. As you master the dynamics of content and process you will discover radical new ideas. I will give you some clear examples of what this looks like and why quality change is dependent on the leader's sophistication in relation to the dynamics of both content and process deliberations. In Chapter 2, for example, you will hear from a deputy high school principal how resistance dissolved when an innovation—peer coaching, in this instance—was worked through in a process where teachers had a chance to help shape the change as they developed capacity and increased ownership. In other cases you will find out why I say "students are radical change

> Crucially, because we are talking about deep change in a superficial situation, you are going to have to break through the status quo without knowing exactly how things will turn out.

agents"—something we did not realize until we delved into Deep Learning.

The third quality consists of managing another productive tension—leading and learning in equal measure. You can never be too sure of yourself, so you always have to be learning. But you also have to be helpful, clear, and decisive along the way. What are the ins and outs of learning and leading simultaneously?

Fourth, a powerful and unanticipated finding from our Deep Learning work is that students of all ages are a hidden source of change leadership. On the one hand they need good pedagogues to help shape their learning (students as protégés), and on the other hand they readily emerge as change agents in terms of pedagogy, learning environment, and social change. We have vastly underestimated what children and youth can do. Our goal is to make them part and parcel of system change.

In another twist, I see student agency as an indirect way of transforming the teaching profession in terms of our powerful concept of *professional capital* (Hargreaves & Fullan, 2012). Professional capital consists of three components: human capital (the quality of the individual), social capital (the quality of the group), and decision capital (the quality of expert judgments). As I discuss in Chapter 4, no "task forces" on transforming the teaching profession have made any difference in the quality of the profession. Students and teachers working together on scale could change the profession more rapidly and deeply. Professional capital is a new currency, and if you increase its circulation, deep change will be the result. Our finding is that students are potentially great agents for increasing the velocity of professional capital and its spread.

The fifth dynamic involves the balancing act of going outward in order to improve inward. You will need to link your organization to the wider system (otherwise your chances of sustainability become seriously compromised, and you will not get your share of good ideas). Your best way of accomplishing this is to contribute to the betterment of the larger system as you gain from it. You need, in other words, to feed and be fed by the system. But what does this mean in practice? I call this "systemness," and you will learn what it means in Chapter 5.

Finally, and paradoxically, the way to sustain the work into the future is for leaders, as essential as they are in the early stages, to deliberately become *dispensable* over time. Sounds like an odd leadership goal, to make yourself less needed, but when you think about it, the best contribution that you can make is to develop individual and collective leadership in others who become capable of carrying on and going further after you leave. You pave the way toward this state through qualities 1 through 5. You consciously work from Day 1 on the proposition "How can I work with depth today in order to make myself dispensable to the future good of this organization?" The answer, which is more ego enhancing than ego smashing, is that I build a culture that has depth. We will examine indicators of depth such as *coherence,* which we define as the "shared depth of understanding about the nature of the work among organizational members" (Fullan & Quinn, 2016). You can't establish permanence by ignoring what might happen after you leave.

In sum, my challenge to the reader is to pose and pursue the question of how you can master all six sets of tensions, for yourself and for those you work with. To do this is to become efficient under complex conditions because as you consciously work on each of the six you are feeding the other five. You end up working on all six simultaneously, thereby achieving cross-cutting efficiencies that make this work possible and deeply engaging for all.

I believe that the timing is right in education for the kind of leadership that I will portray because the cracks in the status quo are becoming ever more visible and intolerable, and the insights we have about the six sets of tensions are coming into focus. Under some circumstances, taking a risk invites martyrdom. Under current scenarios, it's a chance to become a hero. Indelibly speaking, it's a chance to generate many, many heroes who, in turn, spawn others. This book will set you on an irreversible path for deep change. Each chapter will end with a list of three or four action steps. It is time to help yourself and others learn your way into the future, thereby creating a society radically different from the one we have today.

CHAPTER

1

Moral Imperative and Uplifting Leadership

Moral imperative is about meaningfulness in life and work. It consists of a strong internal commitment to accomplish something of significant value. In education, this is often expressed as learning for all students. The new moral imperative, exhibited in this book, is *deep learning* for all students. *Breakthrough* means achieving dramatic results never before accomplished. The reason that I combine moral imperative and uplifting leadership into one phenomenon is that one without the other is empty. Moral imperative is meaningless if it is just on paper and not being enacted. Uplifting leadership needs a purpose; moral imperative involving identity, mastery, creativity, and connectedness fuels the journey. The tension is that moral imperative is sometimes uttered without mobilizing people to enact it. Or people get active without firm goals.

The goal of leadership, then, is to help cause breakthroughs by being part of a process that uplifts large numbers of people. It is to make deep change happen and be meaningful to individuals and the group. To do any good, meaning must have a collective face. In this chapter I want to do two things: first, to define deep meaning and motivation in relation to breakthrough moral imperative, and second, to show how uplifting leadership fits in. This combination is the key overall disposition. Then I will show how the next four tensions—content and process, lead and learn, seeing students as change agents and protégés, and feeding and being fed by the system—turn essential leadership into indelible leadership.

BREAKTHROUGH MORAL IMPERATIVE AND DEEP WORK

There are very few things as basic to human nature as wondering about the meaning of daily existence. So let's start with the fundamentals. Leadership is about helping people find meaning. The action verb here is *to motivate*. We need a succinct and relatively complete definition of what constitutes "motivation for deep learning."

Dan Pink (2009) got us off to a strong start in his book, *Drive*. Pink found that the combination of purpose, mastery, and a degree of autonomy or self-direction was related to higher performance. To this I would add *connectedness*. It is fundamentally human to want to be part of creating something worthwhile with others.

Now we come to the hard part. Mobilizing moral imperative. It would be great to say that if we stoked people's passion we would get lots of new, deep meaning. However, if individuals don't have palpable passion, you could hardly get it by cajoling or otherwise urging them to *be more passionate*. Or take the flip side and ask whether passion is always a good thing. In the Preface, I mentioned Cal Newport's (2016) latest book, *Deep Work*. Newport's previous book was called *So Good They Can't Ignore You* (2012). He shows, for example, that passion without skill can be dangerous, which makes perfect sense when you think about it. He also argues that if you don't have fire in your belly, it may be less helpful to try to fake it (or join a cult) than it would be to develop new, useful skills, thereby discovering your own new passions.

The leadership implications are profound. Yes, leverage passion where you find it (and in some cases, maybe tone it down), but mostly give people (e.g., students) new experiences that lead them to realize passions they did not know they had. Maybe certain people are not passionate at all, but being human, most of us are prone to be drawn into something that is personally and socially meaningful—something in which we could become deeply immersed. In this way, people find new meaning relative to their existence (after all, we are talking about depth).

Locating and activating moral imperative is at the heart of answering Goffee and Jones's (2015) provocative question: Why should anyone work here? Great question for the would-be indelible leader! It won't be sufficient for the leader to convince herself or himself that people should *want* to work here; rather, the litmus test is that many people *become or end up* wanting to do important deep things together. Goffee and Jones did not say "let's start with a strategic plan and attract people to it"; rather, they asked a more basic question: "What will attract people to want to spend their energies in making something worthwhile happen?" When people work in organizations that stand for something specific and valuable, they come to have a sense of identity and commitment to what they are doing. Indeed, people become aware of the significance of the work. As one senior executive expressed it in the Goffee and Jones study, people become conscious of the future, ready "to take positive steps to ensure the permanence and longevity of the company" (p. 105), or perhaps more accurately, people

> Leverage passion where you find it (and in some cases, maybe tone it down), but mostly give people new experiences that lead them to realize passions they did not know they had. Maybe they are not passionate at all, but being human they are drawn to join in and consequently become deeply immersed in and committed to the cause.

become committed to working for a collective cause that is equally individually fulfilling.

> People become committed to working for a collective cause that is equally individually fulfilling.

Deep work and indelible leadership are intertwined, for obvious reasons. When work is deep it has a greater chance of lasting. The challenge, as Cal Newport (2016) shows, is that deep work is increasingly rare. Newport defines deep work as follows:

> Professional activities performed in a state of distraction-free concentration that push your cognitive capacities to their limit. These efforts create new value, improve your skill, and are hard to replicate. (p. 3)

We won't be purist in following this definition; for example, who can be fully distraction-free these days? And my only quibble with the definition is that deep work also requires serious *emotional* capacities. But you get the point. Deep work will require reducing distractors and mobilizing concentration of the group on the moral task at hand. The flip side, "shallow work," is easily recognized in the age of superficiality that I referred to earlier. Newport (2016) puts it this way: "Non-cognitively demanding . . . tasks [are] often performed while distracted. These efforts tend not to create much new value in the world and are easy to replicate" (p. 6).

Newport (2016) supplies a truckload of examples that deep work is becoming more and more rare "at exactly the same time it is becoming increasingly *valuable* in our economy" (p. 14), the latter being my point about the timeliness of indelible leadership. Even when one deliberately tries to track down examples of deep learning, as Mehta

> Deep work will require reducing distractors and mobilizing concentration of the group on the moral task at hand.

and Fine (2015) did, one comes up rather empty. Without question schooling, as we know it, has become increasingly superficial *at the very time that depth is required.* Reversing this trend is the goal of uplifting leadership.

UPLIFTING LEADERSHIP

In the previous section, we saw traces of what uplifting leadership entails. Essentially, it is to mobilize deep action, meaning, and impact on the part of large numbers of individuals and the collectivity. As mentioned earlier, Andy Hargreaves, Alan Boyle, and Alma Harris (2014) have focused on the very topic of uplifting leadership in their study of extraordinary performance in three sectors: business, education, and sports. Here I want to highlight only the concept of uplifting leadership. In education there are many forces keeping things the way they are—traditional and

> Deep leadership enters the arena of what humans *could do* if they mobilized collectively.

ineffective for the times. Later on I will introduce Bruce Dixon's (2015) powerful phrase *legacy pedagogy* and add my own *legacy cultures* to make the point that the status quo is proving enormously resistant to unseat, even though there are many who strongly desire transformation. In big change the problem is that people are not confident in a new radical alternative, partly because they cannot imagine what it might look like and do, and also because they do not have the capacity to pull it off. Our six leadership dispositions, along with the allure of the 6Cs of helping oneself and humanity, I believe are powerful and timely enough to disrupt and redefine the status quo as a new state of affairs. Deep leaders attempt to uplift themselves and others for exactly that purpose. The first steps will be the hardest, but the good news is that there are a surprising number of takers. The push factors (a bad status quo) and the pull factors (exciting pedagogy, global competencies, enabling leadership) form the seeds of a perfect storm.

Timing, the future is now! A profound need conjures up a job description: Wanted, leaders willing to throw themselves into the deep end while they save others and themselves!

I am forecasting an abrupt and deep change in education. Rushkoff (2016) puts it well:

> Big data doesn't tell us what a person *could* do. It tells us what a person will likely do on the past actions of other people. The big rub is that invention of genuinely new products, of game changers, never comes from refining our analysis of existing consumer trends but from stoking the ingenuity of our innovators. (p. 43, italics in original)

> Deep leadership is not about finding things that were always there; it is about creating things that were never imagined.

Deep leadership enters the arena of what humans *could do* if they mobilized collectively. In this book we will find the innovators in the deep end of learning, and many of them are students open to doing things never before conceived. Deep leadership is not about finding things that were always there; it is about creating things that were never imagined. Once identified, once shaped and reshaped, they will form the basis of a new era of radical change in how and what humans learn.

The rest of this book equips you with the mindset and tools you will need to be uplifting in a sea of change: master content and process, lead and listen in equal measure, see students as change agents and protégés, feed and be fed by the system, make yourself essential and dispensable—these are the ingredients of deep leadership. Develop these qualities in yourself and others and you will make a mark of deep improvement while you lead—one that lasts and grows far beyond your tenure.

● ● ● ● ACTION STEPS

1. Reflect on the question "Why should anyone work here?" in relation to your organization. Identify a couple of actions you could take that would make people *want* to invest their time and energy in your organization.

2. To what extent is your organization a place where you and others feel safe to do things differently, fail, learn from failure, and get better as a result? How could you model in public being a lead learner?

3. Have a preliminary discussion around the question "What is deep learning for your group?" With the group, list the opportunities that people have to experience deep learning and to witness deep learning in the students or adults they work with.

4. Realize that you are entering a period of radical innovations. Be open to being surprised and to surprising others with your explorations.

CHAPTER
2

Master Content and Process

Here is the dilemma. You have good ideas as a leader, but there isn't enough take-up. Also your proposals may not be as good as you think they are. To resolve these matters, you have to master both the content of change *and* the process of change as you work through the concepts with others. Our succinct definition of this skill is that all effective change processes shape and reshape ideas as they develop capacity and ownership. The ideas are shaped and reshaped because other people will have additional knowledge and insight about how to improve the solution, and of course you need people's skill and commitment at the same time. Miss either one—due to poor or incomplete refinement of the idea or failure to capture people's commitment—and you will fail. Leaders have to be equally at home in content and process and in their merging. Moreover, as I stated in the previous chapter, radical new ideas are in the offing but not yet imagined. So part of the leadership challenge is to stoke innovators, realizing that almost anyone could be an innovator in waiting.

I get some of the best examples of the content/process dynamics from practitioners who are doing the work with success. We were working in the Australian Capital Territory (ACT) a few years ago with a system of 80 schools that was somewhat stagnant in performance. A number of things were done to jump-start the system, and our example comes from Canberra Secondary School, where leaders had introduced a peer coaching procedure (that I mentioned earlier) in which three teachers were trained in a "quality teaching framework" as peer observers. We were there from the beginning, and most teachers in the school said that they were not interested in participating ("We don't want other teachers coming into our room, observing, and telling us how to teach"). Let's call this resistance. Leaders did a number of good things during the process to address concerns: not being too pushy, refining the procedure, letting people get a taste of what it entails, using peers who were experiencing success to share their stories, identifying examples of impact, and so on. When we next visited the school three years later to do some filming, every teacher in the school was involved in the process. Teachers and students were engaged, learning had improved, and there was a noticeable high energy in the school. At the end of the day of filming, I sat down with the deputy principal who was leading the initiative and observed, "This is impressive. Three years ago there was strong resistance. Now, with most of the same people, everyone is enthusiastically participating and getting results." I then asked him the killer change question: "Is the peer coaching procedure voluntary or mandatory?" Without hesitation, he responded, "It is voluntary but inevitable!"

> An effective change process develops ideas that are voluntary but inevitable.

When you master both the content (revision of good ideas) and the process (skilled participation) change *is* inevitable. The moment you have to rely on mandating a new practice as your main way of getting it to happen is the moment you have gone off track.

Another example of learning as you go comes from David Cote, the chairman and CEO of Honeywell. He was asked by Adam

Bryant what was the most important leadership lesson he had learned in his years of success. Here is what he said:

> I have a reputation for being decisive. Most people would say that being decisive is what you want in a business leader. But it's possible for decisiveness to be a bad thing. Because if you're decisive, you want to make decisions— give me what you've got, and I'll make a decision. . . . But with bigger decisions, you can make bigger mistakes. (Bryant, 2013)

And the lesson:

> There's this phrase I use a lot when I teach leadership classes at Honeywell: Your job as a leader is to be right at the end of the meeting, not at the beginning of the meeting. It's your job to flush out all the facts, all the opinions, and at the end make a good decision, because you'll get measured on whether you made a good decision, and not whether it was your idea from the beginning. (Bryant, 2013)

In other words, if you are right at the beginning of the meeting you are right only in your own mind, whereas if you are right at the end of the meeting you have processed the ideas with the group, listened, sorted out key issues, and arrived at a sense of

"Your job as a leader is to be right at the end of the meeting, not at the beginning of the meeting. It's your job to flush out all the facts, all the opinions, and at the end make a good decision, because you'll get measured on whether you made a good decision, and not whether it was your idea from the beginning." (Bryant, 2013)

what to do next. Of course, the meeting is just a metaphor for a process of focused interaction over a period of time in which people, including the leaders, refine the idea by discussing and testing it out, developing skills, examining meaning and impact. In this way, by the end of the meeting/process you are right with the group. A key part of being a great leader is that you hire and make it clear that you want people who are open minded, cognitively and socially intelligent, and questioning. You want learners who speak up. Then you must help yourself and others process the noise.

How do you get this good? I will elaborate on this point in Chapter 3—lead and learn in equal measure—but for now, we can be clear that leaders must be *learners*. A good example of this concerns the role of school principals. A few years ago, policy makers discovered research that seemed to say that when the principal acts as an "instructional leader" student achievement results go up. This turned out to be one of those dangerous half-truths. When schools systems began to act on this "finding," they required principals to be trained in observation, walkthroughs, and the like and to observe teachers and give feedback. Not a bad idea on the surface, but it was really based on a "being right at the beginning of the meeting" strategy. There weren't enough hours in the day to do all the one-on-ones that were necessary, and when the principal tried to fulfill his or her duties faithfully, it alienated him or her from teachers because it was superficial and much too one-sided.

> A key part of being a great leader is that you hire and make it clear that you want people who are open minded, cognitively and socially intelligent, and questioning.

What the research actually said was more nuanced (toward the theme of this chapter). Viviane Robinson (2011), in her large-scale meta-study of research on what effective principals did, found five factors associated with impact on student achievement school wide. Expressed as statistical effect sizes, she found that effective school leaders focused on the following:

1. Establishing goals and expectations (effect size 0.42)

2. Resourcing strategically (0.31)

3. Ensuring quality teaching (0.42)

4. Leading teaching and learning development (0.84)

5. Ensuring an orderly and safe environment (0.27)

Note that "Leading teaching and learning development" stands out as substantially more powerful than any of the other four domains. When you examine Robinson's finding in detail, you discover that the actions pertaining to this factor involve "participating as a learner" with teachers in moving the school forward. Think of it this way: a first-year school principal does many of the right things (items 1, 2, 3, and 5) but does not participate as a learner the first five years of her or his career. In this case, the person will know about as much in year 5 as he or she did in year 1 (five times nothing is nothing!). On the other hand, the principal who does participate as a learner with teachers, strangely enough, does learn. She or he learns with and from teachers (and, as we shall see, learns from students) and, indeed, gets better and better. I would venture to say that if a principal becomes immersed as a learner, she or he will also get better at the other four items on Robinson's list.

In fact, the leader who really becomes knowledgeable will have to be careful because she or he might become too confident (bossy) or followers can become too readily accepting of recommendations made by the leader. David Cote, our being "right at the end of the meeting" guy, recognized this problem:

> I've also had to think about the kind of people I put around me. If I'm very decisive and I surround myself with people who just want me to make decisions, then we'll go off the cliff at 130 miles an hour, because at some point I'll be wrong. What I need are people who want to come to their own conclusions and are willing to think independently, and can argue with me in the right way so that I will internalize it and keep it objective. (Bryant, 2013)

Once again, we see that people who raise questions are crucial to learning and that leaders need to foster the dynamic of diverse ideas and integration. Because we are addressing deep work in this book, which by definition involves new solutions, there is a lot to learn; in fact, there is a lot to discover and create. In the deep learning world, innovations never before conceived are being generated. You cannot possibly access and process knowledge by yourself—information that is massively available but often undigested. Furthermore, in deep learning we are talking about innovations that are being developed for the first time, making it essential that leaders listen and learn as they lead.

In this new world, you need the group for two reasons: you need their ideas, and you need to lead a process of shaping and reshaping the content of possible solutions. As a leader, you have to be best at mastering new content and dynamic processes. People will have a lot of anxieties and questions but also great energy and commitment if you can arrive at regular breakthroughs. You do not have to be the most knowledgeable content person in the room (in fact, you won't be), but you do have to help ensure that the group's ideas are accessed and processed.

> You do not have to be the most knowledgeable content person in the room (in fact, you won't be), but you do have to help ensure that the group's ideas are accessed and processed.

As Joanne Quinn and I argued, coherence is fully and only *subjective* (Fullan & Quinn, 2016). This means that just because you, as a leader, have focus and are clear doesn't mean the larger group is clear. And maybe your clarity needs to be disturbed by the ideas of others. Coherence is subjective, and shared coherence is the name of the game. You have to shape ideas and interactions over time to arrive at best outcomes. Coherence is based on the shared depth of understanding in the group about the nature of the (new) work. Coherence-making, incidentally, is never done—you get new ideas, people come and go, the environments changes, results are not forthcoming, and so on. There are no shortcuts to deep learning, but once the processes are in train, you will have increased your coherence-making capacity.

CONNECTIONS FORWARD

This is the time to remind the reader that, thankfully, every one of the six leadership factors serves the other five. Thus when it comes to mastering content and process you have considerable help. The focus on moral imperative and uplifting leadership contributes ideas and commitment. Learn and lead, to which we will turn in a moment, obviously centers on both content and process. Seeing students as change agents and protégés improves pedagogy and professional capital. Feeding and being fed by the system necessarily places you in a bigger arena, without which you could not garner the best ideas or build the relationships that would be helpful for sustaining your organization. Lastly, you will have to be reminded that at the end of the day, you had better become dispensable—you will have worked all the while in the other five leadership domains to establish the conditions for others to keep on learning beyond your tenure.

● ● ● ● ACTION STEPS

1. Write down in a single paragraph *what* the core improvement work of your organization is about. Be specific.

2. To what extent is there "a shared depth of understanding about the nature of the work" in your organization? Can people "talk the walk" in specific and consistent ways?

3. How easy is it for you to name evidence of "being right at the end of the meeting"? What practices could you incorporate in your everyday work to increase the frequency and depth of opportunities for people to provide feedback and shape the organization's change ideas?

CHAPTER
3

Lead and Learn in Equal Measure

Why "equal" measure? Two reasons: first, there is a lot more to be learned these days, especially as you go deeper into the unknown. Listening and learning, which are the mark of effective leaders, all too often are missing. In the modern world they are crucial. The second reason is that members depend on leaders to help make sense of new, deep work. Leaders will not be able to take up this role effectively if they are not participating as learners with a special responsibility to make sense of new developments while feeding this back to organizational members. The purpose of feedback is partly to test whether the leader is getting an accurate read on the situation and partly to move the group forward into doing more of the new, right thing while focusing on assessing impact. In complex situations, leaders listen and learn *so that they can lead better*.

NEW LEADERSHIP IN ACTION

We especially see these new leadership developments in our Deep Learning initiative (www.npdl.global). I said earlier that traditional schooling is boring and also not very useful for life in the 21st century. In my book *Stratosphere* (Fullan, 2013), I argued that the solution must integrate three forces: technology, pedagogy, and change knowledge (the latter being the subject of *Indelible Leadership*). I also noticed that some teachers, principals, and their students were taking naturally to exploring radical alternatives—giving me faith in the inevitability of human evolution (the idea that human nature corrects itself over time).

My colleagues and I decided to leverage this desire for a solution by establishing a focused network of clusters of schools and their systems as a real-time laboratory of development and dissemination. The "pedagogies" part involves new learning partnerships between and among students, teachers, and families engaged in Deep Learning that fosters the global competencies—the 6Cs that I described earlier (character, citizenship, collaboration, communication, creativity, and critical thinking). We are capturing what this looks like in practice as we help to stimulate with rubrics and other tools to guide and assess the 6Cs. The tools focus the work and shape deliberations about what to do and how to assess (learn from) what is happening. As I mentioned, there are currently more than 700 schools involved from seven different countries.

It should be obvious that the success of Deep Learning requires a new kind of leadership—leadership for deep work. We are seeing and facilitating many examples of this work in action and are just now beginning to document what it looks like. Deep work, by definition, means that we don't know exactly what it should look like until we do it. This requires a very different kind of leadership. Some of our preliminary findings are listed in the following box.

New Leadership for Deep Work

- Cycles of trying things and making meaning
- Co-learning (among all) dominates
- Leaders listen, learn, ask questions
- Leaders help crystallize, articulate, and feed back what they see
- Leaders act on emerging solutions, including the focus on impact

At first, the leader is very much a co-learner. They "participate as learners," beginning to articulate what they see happening and listening to feedback. Leaders really have to work at extracting the meaning and value of what they are seeing because participants are not necessarily all that clear about what they are doing and what it amounts to. Leaders need to probe—"tell me more about what you just said, what you meant by it." Put another way, at the early stages leaders ask a lot more questions than they have answers for. As you go you must cumulatively become one of the main "meaning makers." When you are acting this way you will see a range of actions and activities, and as a purposeful learner you will learn to make sense of new potential breakthroughs. You will see how things fit that others don't necessarily see. But the ultimate test of your accuracy is not whether *you* can make sense of what you are seeing but whether your leading observations are a revelation to those working on the issues. In a real sense you are a purveyor of "making the light bulb go off in many heads." In deep work, people know that they are onto something big, but in the early stages they can't quite put their finger on what it is or how it might become better. The new leaders are good "finger putters" as they help accelerate that process (and help develop other leaders who can do the same). Deep leaders are also conscious of impact. They are open to new measures, but they want to know—more accurately, they want the group to know—what actions are producing deep results: engaged learners who are developing global competencies such as the 6Cs. They are less concerned about accountability per se (although, paradoxically, they get more of it with this approach) and more focused on individual and collective efficacy.

> At the early stages, leaders ask a lot more questions than they have answers for.

I captured some of this in an interview with John Malloy, one of our Ontario leaders engaged deeply in this work. John was, until recently, director (superintendent) of the Hamilton Wentworth District School Board (HWDSB) just west of Toronto. In the last half of 2015, John moved into the Ontario government as chief student achievement officer, but then he was abruptly recruited on an emergency assignment as director of the troubled Toronto District School Board and its more than 500 schools. HWDSB is one of our Deep Learning school districts. They started with 14 of their 104 schools in Deep Learning. Six months *after* John departed, HWDSB leadership decided to develop Deep Learning in all of its 104 schools—what we call a whole system approach. I italicize "after" to highlight indelible leadership. Here is a leader whose system carries on and deepens the work after he leaves. In one way he was a champion of the work, but more fundamentally he obviously helped deepen it for many others. Not quite indelible but a pretty good "stain."

> You are a purveyor of "making the light bulb go off in many heads."

So, how do leaders like John go about their work? He started the interview with these words:

> The more senior we are in this hierarchy, the greater the expectation is that we can articulate what we are doing, why we are doing it, how we are going to measure it, and when we are going to be able to communicate the outcomes. (J. Malloy, personal communication, November 2015)

John was implying that if you stay in this "having to have the answers" role you will be stuck in the status quo. He went on to say that if you are to break new ground, "you've got to be willing to take risks." And then he identified how *disciplined* this work must be:

> The next piece that's important is that there has to be—and this is the language I use—vehicles, protocols, processes to actually reflect upon the learning, to make meaning out of what is emerging from the learning and then articulate from that. We did check ins every month with a number of the different processes that were happening in these schools so that we could understand what's happening, both for the teachers and the students, how do we know, what does what we're learning mean for our practice and what does it mean for how we are talking about learning in Hamilton.
>
> So my job became, let's engage in the learning discussion at the senior table based upon all the superintendents who are working with principals and teachers so that we can come to some articulation. And we did that. So that we were continuously informing the way in which the narrative was evolving, so that's how we made meaning. (J. Malloy, personal communication, November 2015)

And further:

> I spent quite a bit of time learning and listening to the teachers and the principals who were engaged in [Deep Learning]. So, in other words, I went to their sessions and became a participant, and that really allowed me to leverage, to broker and to make that coherent meaning because I could then not speak for me. I just spent a day with the teachers who were working on this process, working with the tools, the rubric and so forth, and this is what I saw. Like you're doing right now, I'd walk around and I'd ask some probing questions to help me understand so, what is the most the significant thing that has happened in your practice? What happened to your students?

I continuously loop back, not only to the schools, but also to the senior team to create coherence around what's our direction. (J. Malloy, personal communication, November 2015)

Even though deep work involves unknown territory, we can see for people like John Malloy that it is a disciplined process. It is bound to sort out what is being learned. Innovations must eventually become more precise so that people know exactly what they look like and do. Specificity does not have to mean imposition; rather, it means clarity about practice and its impact.

> Specificity does not have to mean imposition; rather, it means clarity about practice and its impact.

Because specificity is always being pursued and tested, and because all leaders are involved in this grounded process, you end up with a good deal of shared clarity about the nature of the work. When good new work becomes this widely shared, backed up by layers of leaders, it can survive (indeed, go beyond) the departure of leaders as good as John Malloy.

To return to Cal Newport, he is not just making the case for "deep work" but is saying that current conditions favor "shallow work."

> Breakthrough leadership consists of a process of focused attention with others on the evolution of new work, asking questions, giving and getting specific feedback.

Multiple initiatives, minute-by-minute distractions, and the ease of staying superficially with the status quo all conspire to keep us in the state of inertia (we keep on doing what we are already doing). New deep work will require intense concentration and participation of the kind we saw with John Malloy, to encourage and be part of radical new ways of working. Thus breakthrough leadership consists of a process of focused attention with others on the evolution of new work, asking questions, giving and getting specific feedback. In Newport's (2016) words:

To learn hard things quickly, you must focus intensely without distraction. To learn . . . is an act of deep work. If you are comfortable going deep, you'll be comfortable mastering the increasingly complex systems and skills needed to thrive in our economy. If you instead remain one of the many for whom depth is uncomfortable and distraction ubiquitous, you shouldn't expect these systems and skills to come easily to you. (p. 37)

GOING DEEPER AND BIGGER

Deep work is rare, and it's difficult, but it is also learnable and rewarding. Newport (2016) associates this work with concepts we have already made central to indelible leadership, such as "meaningfulness." Human beings "are at their best when immersed deeply in something challenging . . . the act of going deep orders the consciousness in a way that makes life [work] worthwhile" (pp. 84–85). Note also that deep work involves growing mastery (of complex situations) that is another vein that makes life worth living. Speaking personally, I find the greatest satisfaction in our "whole system" work to be solving complex problems that make a difference in the lives of tens of thousands of teachers and students. The solving of a difficult societal problem is perhaps more gratifying than the impact itself.

We have one more lens to help position deep transformational system change. Roger Martin and Sally Osberg (2015) studied how successful social entrepreneurs accomplished large-scale system change. Their findings resonate with our analyses. They acknowledge, as we have just seen with Newport, that new or emergent fields (read: deep work) are amorphous at the beginning, and thus "it is no easy feat to productively reflect on something that is not yet well-defined and rapidly changing" (p. 6). Martin and Osberg's goal is to understand the process of "social transformation":

Positive, fundamental, and lasting change to the prevailing conditions under which most members of a society live and work. (p. 32)

Sounds like deep indelible change to me! Getting to my point about timeliness (in my case, relative to educational change), Martin and Osberg (2015) observe that mostly current equilibrium is widely accepted, even if some people are unhappy with it. But, "every once in a while, backed by revolutionary rather than normal thinking, a society leaps forward to a fundamental new equilibrium" (p. 37). My book essentially argues that for learning and education, now is one of those "every once in a while" times.

When Martin and Osberg (2015) zero in on leadership they are talking our language. They begin by saying that one has to understand, and be immersed in, a particular status quo before starting to change it. Then to have any chance of transforming the system, you have to engage with certain tensions or dilemmas. For example, to simply criticize a system and propose an alternative will not have much of an impact. As I sometimes put it, "being right is not a strategy" (or, if you like, being right at the beginning of the meeting will not cut it). The threefold framework of grappling with specific big dilemmas offered by Martin and Osberg is fundamentally congruent with the points that I have been making:

> Being right is not a strategy.

- Abhorrence and appreciation of the status quo

- Expertise and apprenticeship

- Experimentation and commitment (Martin & Osberg, 2015)

Relative to the first distinction, they found that "the most successful change agents . . . must manage to both abhor the existing conditions and appreciate the system that produces them" (p. 84). As leaders understand what makes the existing situation tick, they begin to design transformational solutions. That is exactly what we are doing with Deep Learning (although in our work, I have slightly changed the first equation to "reject and respect" the status quo).

The second tension is "expertise and apprenticeship." Specifically this means that the leader has expertise in some domains, but she or he must be a learner (apprentice to those who know more in other respects). This is precisely how John Malloy was leading in HWDSB. Moreover, in our latest work in Deep Learning we are finding that teachers and administrators must, in certain respects, become learners (apprentices) to students (Fullan, 2015c). This is quite radical, but then again so is transformation. We are currently mining our data to identify scores of examples in which students are the agent of change—in pedagogy, in the organization, and relative to societal changes.

Again, Martin and Osberg (2015) nail it:

> The social entrepreneur will also learn to draw on the wisdom of those not seen or classified as experts, especially those living within the system, in order to gain insights about their beliefs and practices. Instead of deferring to the prevailing wisdom embraced by those who benefit from the status quo, of whom he may well be one, the social entrepreneur positions himself to absorb lessons from ecosystem actors, especially those most disadvantaged by the existing equilibrium. (p. 92)

The third tension is "experimentation and commitment." Experiments are not just temporary trials. They are designed so that leaders learn something from what is tried. New knowledge and commitment can be accumulated. The key is to keep going, building on what is being learned. This is very much what we are seeing in Hamilton and other Deep Learning jurisdictions: Learn from what is happening by observing, probing, extracting, and testing as you help articulate and consolidate commitment to the good practices and ideas that are emerging.

Indelible leadership is not just changing practices of the corner store or the isolated school here and there. It is fundamentally a matter of *system transformation*. As is well stated by Martin and Osberg (2015),

> Social entrepreneurs . . . must articulate their winning aspirations, and do so in the context of transformative change.

They must go beyond simply articulating an improvement to the system even if the improvement is clearly a laudatory one. (p. 110)

And then Martin and Osberg draw the fundamental conclusion:

Social entrepreneurs are driven to get beyond better. The social entrepreneur's vision must speak definitively to the new, transformed societal equilibrium she is prepared to bring about: it must be aimed at equilibrium change rather than at the amelioration of current conditions; it must be specific yet systemic in its approach, targeted at a constituency that cannot effect the change alone [in our case, students cannot effect the change alone] while also considering the system holistically; finally more often than not, it must be adaptable and resilient in the face of changing conditions. (p. 110)

Now that's a revolution! Martin and Osberg's last point is that the revolution is not over once you seem to be able to declare victory. There will always be changing conditions, all the more so once a new state is emerging.

> The learning can never be over.

Indelible leadership is a forever proposition because conditions and people are always changing. In a phrase, the learning can never be over.

THE SUBTLETIES OF INNOVATION AND CREATIVITY

Innovation and creativity are essential because deep learning implies finding novel ways to break into radically new territory. First, we can "back into" new creativity, or innovative ways of thinking, by noting that despite the need for relentless focus, we also need to step back sometimes to allow new ideas to percolate (the old idea that one often gets the best ideas in the shower). Although Newport (2016) stresses the need for leaders to focus in order to go deep, and to avoid annoying distractions, he also makes the case for periodically getting away from intensity. As he puts it, often we need to "take a break from focus" (p. 159). This makes perfect sense. When doing deep work, trying to solve difficult problems, and coming up with solutions, you need to cycle back and forth between periods of intensity and occasions when you get away from direct problem solving and engage in mediation, relaxation, and simply doing nothing. Deep work does require coming up with ideas that nobody has considered before, or seeing certain things in a new light, and the like.

We see many facets of this focus-retreat-refocus phenomenon in Kaufman and Gregoire's (2016) *Wired to Create: Unraveling the Mysteries of the Creative Mind.* A quote from Picasso captures this unpredictable process: "A painting is not thought out and settled in advance. While it is being done, it changes as one's thoughts change. And when finished, it goes on changing, according to the state of mind of whoever is looking at it" (pp. xiv–xv). Thus deep work changes as you do it, and when you arrive at some consolidation it will keep on changing in some ways. Continuous creation and recreation is part and parcel of the process.

Needless to say the whole process is tricky, embodying a number of noise factors, many of which turn out to be valuable. Our framework (see Figure 1 in the Author's Note) provides guidelines and anchors along the way, but expect some "necessary messiness" as you go.

> Deep work changes as you do it, and when you arrive at some consolidation it will keep on changing in some ways.

Kaufman and Gregoire (2016) show that the creativity journey is nonlinear, with a lot of jumping around on the way to settled outcomes. It is not that the creative leader *stays confused* but that confusion in the early stages of something complex and new is normal. The leader does not know how something is going to turn out until he or she and the group eventually *make it turn out.* Kaufmann and Gregoire first identify the characteristic *messy minds*: "constant toggling between imaginative and rational ways of thinking" (p. xix). They summarize:

The common strand that seemed to transcend all creative fields was an openness to one's inner life, a preference for complexity and ambiguity, an unusually high tolerance for disorder and disarray, the ability to extract order from chaos, independence, unconventionality, and a willingness to take risks. (p. xxiii)

I am not suggesting that leaders should deliberately get confused, but in the course of going deeper they should appreciate a degree of complexity and mystery in what is being attempted by themselves and others in the group. Kaufmann and Gregoire (2016) summarize what they call the "super factors of personality that highly correlate with creativity: plasticity, divergence, and convergence" (p. xxv). Or, if you like, explore and engage, independent thinking, and precision of resolution.

Kaufman and Gregoire (2016) explore what they call the many paradoxes of the creative process: "mindfulness and mind wandering, openness and sensitivity, solitude and collaboration, play and seriousness, and intuition and reason" (p. xxxiv).

> Deep work will necessitate a certain amount of letting go (of oneself and the group) and hence a degree of doubt and confusion.

I am not offering these ideas as a list for leaders to try and emulate but more to encourage the reader to realize that deep work requires innovation and will necessitate a certain amount of letting go (of oneself and the group) and hence a degree of doubt and confusion. This is why the listening and learning combination is essential. The other factors in our indelible leadership framework also serve both to stimulate divergence and to rein in convergence. The framework operates as a "checks and balances" set of processes: moral imperative steers, uplifting leadership inspires but also holds people accountable, lead and learn both opens us to and closes in on good ideas, and so on. The end result is that more people are working on the deep problems so identified, generating more original ideas, and becoming individually and collectively committed to finding and implementing deep solutions. In a summary statement, Kaufman and Gregoire (2016) say,

> We must make tasks more meaningful and relevant to their personal goals and identity. To foster creativity, it is important to build people's confidence and competence to learn new information and deal with adversity; to make tasks conducive to flow by engaging them in the appropriate level of challenges; and help them develop supportive, positive social relationships. (p. xxxii)

In the first instance, my message is to legitimize risk taking for leaders at all levels of the system. If there was ever a time to take a chance, this is it. In many ways, allowing the losing status quo to persist is the greatest risk any leader could take. In other words, it is better to face the problem of controlling innovation than boredom.

To consolidate in a small way at this juncture in the book: Yes, leading and listening invites a lot of new noise into the equation; some of that noise confuses and can resemble chaos; the skilled leader "leads and learns," thereby helping to identify, articulate, and arrive at new solutions; inspired people generate more novel ideas and work harder to implement them. A new order emerges with insights sometimes occurring abruptly (the light bulb moment). In the next chapter, we turn to an example from education: What kind of leadership do we need to see students as change agents as well as protégés, thereby transforming the teaching profession as it makes Deep Learning a reality for students?

> In the first instance, my message is to legitimize risk taking for leaders at all levels of the system.

● ● ● ● ACTION STEPS

1. Are you good at learning from others? What practices do you, and could you, incorporate to learn alongside people in your organization?

2. Are you pushing into Deep Learning? If so, how? Remember, traditional schooling is boring and not very useful for life in the 21st century.

3. What protocols and practices could you incorporate to help people get new insights—to enable "the light bulb to go off" in many heads, not just your own?

4. How do you pull together what is being learned? How do you help the organization assess the impact of what is being learned? Do you feel empowered to take the risk of engaging in messiness on the way to new breakthroughs?

CHAPTER

4

See Students as Change Agents and Protégés

In this chapter, I am going to "back into" the phenomenon of students as change agents and protégés, which makes them life-long learners capable of helping themselves and humanity. For the latter to thrive, we need pedagogues who, in our terminology, constantly circulate and develop professional capital (Hargreaves & Fullan, 2012). So, how about a problem that requires deep work but so far has defied it? I have a prime candidate: the teaching profession in the United States. My tiny book can put only a dent in the matter as I work through the following sequence: What recommendations have been made over the past three decades to "transform" the teaching profession? What can we make of the fact that these "deep" proposals have had little impact? (The very least we can conclude is that these largely consistent transformational proposals must, by dint of their repeated failure, represent prima facie the *wrong strategy*.) What powerful alternative might there be, and what does it have to do with students?

There have been several high-level attempts to improve the teaching profession. Ironically, they have turned out to be an exercise in going backward. I won't be able to solve the teaching transformation matter in this chapter, but I can provide better direction: first by showing what is wrong with existing solutions and second by offering a fundamentally more powerful alternative, including a "secret ingredient" that could become the most powerful force of all. The start of this chapter may seem far removed from our Deep Learning solution, but be patient. We find our way with a vengeance to the Deep Learning agenda.

THE SORRY PROFESSION

What began as a call to arms in *A Nation at Risk* (National Commission on Excellence in Education, 1983) turned into a thirty-year "war of words" (1986–2016, so far), starting with the Carnegie Report. In May 1986, the Carnegie Forum on Education and the Economy released a national report with the uplifting title *A Nation Prepared: Teachers for the 21st Century.* Among other things, the report offered a "new framework" that included "balancing autonomy and accountability," "schools where professionals teach," "standards for teacher education," "the school as a collegium and the role of lead teachers," "make teachers' salaries and career opportunities competitive," "mobilize the nation's resources to prepare minority youngsters for teaching careers," and so on. Remember, this was thirty years ago! It is only slight exaggeration to say that *nothing happened* as a result—certainly, the profession continued to deteriorate.

Slow forward another decade and another manifesto appears: *What Matters Most: Teaching for America's Future,* a report of the National Commission on Teaching and America's Future (1996). Five big recommendations were offered:

1. Get serious about standards for both students and teachers.

2. Reinvent teacher preparation and professional development.

3. Fix teacher recruitment and put qualified teachers in every classroom.

4. Encourage and reward teacher knowledge and skill.

5. Create schools that are organized for student and teacher success. (p. 64)

Then in 2001, Carnegie tried its hand at teacher education with the premise that "the quality of the teaching corps that is produced will largely determine the success or failure of our public education system and affect the future of democracy for years to come" (p. 1). Things continued to get worse. Teacher satisfaction plummets; teachers warn siblings, cousins, and friends not to enter the profession; the performance of the system declines. This sorry state and history of the teaching profession is insightfully analyzed chapter and verse by Jal Mehta in his book *The Allure of Order: High Hopes, Dashed Expectations, and the Troubled Quest to Remake American Schooling* (2013). As Mehta so well reveals, despite the good ideas about collaboration and focus, the policy agenda got hijacked by those who insisted that increased external "standards and accountability" was the only way to get system improvement—a strategy that Mehta understates as "a weak technology to produce the outcomes policy makers seek" (p. 7).

Mehta parodies No Child Left Behind as

> External accountability [where] a higher power asks a lower power to do something that neither the higher power nor the lower power knows how to do and then proceeds to publicly embarrass the lower power for failing to achieve it. (p. 260)

Today, Mehta and his colleagues are forging forward in a proposal called *From Quicksand to Solid Ground: Building a Foundation to Support Quality Teaching* (Mehta, Theisin-Homer, Braslow, & Lopatin, 2015). I see another national task force brewing. Mehta, armed with his detailed analysis of what does go wrong at the policy level, makes three broad recommendations:

1. Build an R&D (Research and Development) system. (To produce, vet, disseminate, and get into use knowledge about quality teaching)

2. Build the social learning system. (Vertically aligned pathways, school-based learning à la "teaching hospitals," support school and district leaders, develop environments that prioritize learning for adults)

3. Build the policy and political system. (Attractive recruitment, more minority teachers, create career ladders, build next generation competencies and school models to support next generation teaching)

I see no reason why these proposals will resolve the problem in time. For one thing, they are too far removed from direct impact. Second, more hijacking of the agenda is likely: as Mehta (2013) himself observed, *"failed professionalism breeds external rationalization"* (p. 28, italics in original). Instead, we need a more powerful, direct, attractive, understandable, and indeed uplifting approach that will mobilize scores of people to "go deep." The next two sections tackle this problem—transforming the teaching profession—a challenge that has defied all solutions over the past three decades. They are my attempt to end the thirty-year war on the teaching profession, which is, in fact, a war on children.

LEARN HOW TO CIRCULATE PROFESSIONAL CAPITAL

Andy Hargreaves and I laid out the substance and direction of a deep solution that we called *Professional Capital: Transforming Teaching in Every School* (2012). We called the wrong strategy "business capital," which attempts to manufacture quality through minimal investment, external monitoring, seeking to get the most out of *existing* human capital that comes and goes at rapid rates. Our alternative for deep, lasting benefit is professional capital that consists of three interrelated forces: human capital (the quality of the individual), social capital (the quality of the group), and decision capital (the expert judgment and use of evidence). We showed how just focusing on human capital (even good versions) was ineffective in the face of cultures and systems that limit opportunities to innovate. With human capital as your only weapon, the system eats up individuals faster than you can produce them. Second, we marshaled considerable evidence that supported the idea that schools where teachers collaborated in specific ways over time were able to mobilize the collective efforts of teachers to improve the learning of all students. To do this work well requires growing and deepening the decisional expertise of professionals to take the most effective decisions on the spot as well as cumulatively. We put it this way:

> Making decisions in complex situations is what professionalism is all about. The pros do this all the time. They come to have competence, judgment, insight, inspiration, and the capacity for improvisation as they strive for exceptional performance. They do this when nobody is looking, and they do it through and with their colleagues and the team. They exercise their judgments and decisions with collective responsibility, openness to feedback, and willing transparency. They are not afraid to make mistakes as long as they learn from them. They have pride in their work. They are respected by peers and by the public for knowing what they are doing. They strive to outdo themselves and each other in a spirit of making greater individual and collective contributions. (Hargreaves & Fullan, 2012, p. 5)

Social capital—working together in focused, specific ways to learn from others to accomplish something of value—attracts and promotes human capital that, in turn, further develops the group. If we add decisional capital—the ability of individuals and groups to make expert diagnoses and identify corresponding solutions based on experience and expertise—we have the full power of professional capital. The three capitals work together in a virtuous circle to embed the kind of "social learning system" that Mehta advocates. We believe that widespread and deep *professional capital* represents the best bet for transforming the teaching profession in lasting ways. For this to happen, it has to be fostered simultaneously at all levels: school and community, district, across schools and districts, and within policy. Herein lies the rub. We won't accomplish this through another national or super-national task force. We can, however, identify the pieces and building blocks.

I have shown how school principals as "lead leaders" can promote professional capital in schools and obtain great teacher and student results (Fullan, 2014). Many districts have based their success on professional capital strategies (we are just completing four case studies of such districts). We have also seen a strong take-up in California by the whole system as that massive state moves from compliance to capacity building with new strategies and metrics for success. More broadly, Hargreaves and I are receiving countless examples from people who have, on their own, been developing professional capital solutions. We also see the makings of mobilizing teachers themselves as change agents in such initiatives as Ontario's Teacher Learning and Leadership Program, in which teachers themselves lead change, working with other teachers and administrators (Campbell, Lieberman, & Yashkina, 2015).

In short, professional capital could be a center of gravity solution, but it won't be strong enough to prevail unless we combine other powerful elements embedded in my book. For starters, the idea of professional capital appeals to all levels of the system. It is powerful and synergistic and represents a fundamental solution. But we need something else that will unleash professional capital as a ubiquitous force. The best analogy I can think of is Rushkoff's (2016) discussion of "the speed of money." He observes, as others have, that too much capital is concentrated (read "stuck") in the hands of individuals and corporations. As such, it does not circulate and, in effect, becomes "dead money." To be useful, capital must continuously circulate. Rushkoff then considers various ideas for increasing "the velocity of money," making money "a verb," as he puts it.

> We have too much dead professional capital.

We don't have to solve the money problem, but the analogy is perfect. We have too much dead professional capital in education. Professional capital, as Hargreaves and I observed (2012), is valuable only if it circulates. When it circulates, the very process makes it stronger (people learn from each other). As I said above, there have been high-profile attempts since at least 1986 to stir professional capital that remains relatively stagnant to this day. The status quo prevails time and time again, even when there are pockets of interest in changing it.

So far, our professional capital concept has been widely endorsed, but alas there has been not been widespread traction. We need a movement, when up to this point we only have a good idea with differential impact. We need an additional "tipping point" that will serve as a catalyst for professional capital in its deepest sense to circulate. That tipping point, my so-called "secret ingredient," has been under our noses all the time.

THE SECRET INGREDIENT

Bruce Dixon (2016), in his book *The End of School as We Know It,* states, "the cost of ignoring 'legacy pedagogy' is severe" (p. 10). Legacy pedagogy consists of ingrained ways of teaching with the teacher at the center. One could equally talk about "legacy cultures"—established ways of relating to each other. In fact, the previous section of this chapter describes the legacy culture at work. The power of legacies is that they are hard to change *even if* individuals desire the change. People either slip back into the old way of doing things or don't have the clarity, confidence, and/or skill to act in the new way. This takes us back to our main theme, leadership for deep change. Two things are needed: working on deep change itself while having leadership from many quarters that could possibly overcome the legacies that Dixon so accurately worries about.

Believe it or not, our secret ingredient for transforming the teaching profession toward professional capital is *the student as change agent!* Not by themselves but in a rather indirect and surprising way. To get at this, we need to return to our Deep Learning work with the 700-plus schools. We are gathering our initial findings, so we are still at the early stage, but we are seeing some surprising developments. The gist of the kind of leadership that upsets the status quo is that the process might begin by leaders opening the door (a culture of yes), but the real change is when it is taken up spontaneously by teachers and *especially* by students.

I don't mean that students will literally lead the charge to change the profession. But what we are seeing in our work is radical change in pedagogy that will *in effect* transform the profession. Quite directly, students and teachers can turn professional capital into a verb! They can cause it

> Our secret ingredient for transforming the teaching profession toward professional capital is *the student as change agent!*

to circulate within and among schools where it will become better (deeper and more effective) and rapidly (relative to the stagnation of the past three decades) a widespread force for deep learning. Let's call it the "cascading up" theory of action (I know cascading up is impossible, but, then again, so is transforming the teaching profession).

I have already observed that boredom in traditional schooling is trending. As students become less and less interested in schools, teachers, especially young ones, find the profession more and more unappealing. The situation is ripe for change and hence is susceptible to Deep Learning solutions. We started with a definition and a few tools. New pedagogies, as I said, consists of a *learning partnership* between and among students, teachers, and

> New pedagogies, as I said, consists of a *learning partnership* between and among students, teachers, and families.

families (all the ideas, as I said, are not brand-new, but they are new on scale for regular schools). The tools are rubrics and guides related to the global competencies (character, citizenship, collaboration, communication, creativity, and critical thinking), to the learning conditions and culture at the school and community level, and to the environment and context for learning at the regional and national levels. The take-up comes from ordinary schools and districts/municipalities. At the beginning we see some hesitancy or ambivalence to act on the part of educators, even those willing to pursue it. The saving grace is students, who seem to have little trouble staring the status quo in the face. As action unfolds, it is clear that we are participating in a movement, not just a program change. Now, about eighteen months after the onset, we are beginning to gather initial data that I report here in a few snippets from Australia, Canada, and Uruguay, where groups of 100 or more schools in each country are going for Deep Learning. We have completed several case studies that will soon be available. The results should be treated with caution as they represent early stages, but the trends are unmistakable because they are happening all over. In the next paragraphs, I work from the students back to teachers, administrators, and others.

It is a bold statement and more of a projection than a conclusion to say that the strongest forces arising are students as change agents in three respects:

1. Students as agents for pedagogical change in teachers
2. Students as agents of organizational change in schools
3. Students as agents of societal change helping humanity

In a word, it is becoming more and more obvious that students are the world's most underutilized change agents in education.

Here are some examples:

A high school student asked her teacher if she could use a new computer software program to pursue her own assignment in creating a 3-D digital sculpture. With some hesitancy, because this involved a skill set beyond her own, the teacher allowed it and then reflected later as she assessed the outcome that it was a pivotal moment in her shift in understanding of her traditional role as "teacher" (i.e., being responsible for delivering knowledge and designing tasks that ensure mastery) to that of a "co-learner," learning alongside her students and acknowledging her role in providing awareness of and access to the skills and tools that support students in their learning journey.

In a science class, students share feedback with their teacher about the way group work is organized. They tell her that

(Continued)

(Continued)

having people assigned to groups by the teacher is not working too well for them, and they suggest trying out an alternative: students choosing and creating their own groups. The teacher agrees, and the process next time is organized following students' suggestions. In addition to their attention to the task at hand, students and the teacher alike keep an eye on how this new way to create groups is working, and they decide to use what they learn about the process to inform future decisions on group dynamics that best enhance learning in the group.

A school in Australia built its learning around what they called "enigma missions"—complex problems or issues to be solved: One group studied autism because they knew people who were autistic; another took up the issue of homelessness; still another tackled DNA, which a boy observed is an enigma in itself. The students were incredibly engaged and came up with great insights. One student who had studied homelessness and drew some important conclusions said, "I feel so complete"—not in the sense of being done but having brought something valuable to fruition. Having produced great video vignettes displaying exciting learning, students and teachers together reviewed what they had done and concluded that, so far, they were just scratching the surface.

In Uruguay, schools were given simple robotic kits with instructions via YouTube. The kits sat on the shelf until one day the students (10 years old) asked the teacher if they could start to use them. Quickly they created the following: One group was studying World War II and built a device that could detect land mines; another group solved the problem of birds eating vegetables from the garden by building a simple robot that vibrated when birds came near; a third group took up the issue that five people were killed by lightning on a beach, so they built a device that could detect imminent lightning and sound an alarm. One 10-year-old observed, "I am supposed to help humanity, so I decided to start in my own neighborhood." The teacher later observed that the experience caused her to want to change the way she taught.

In a Canadian school, students came home and talked about their inquiries with their families, with parents sometimes getting directly involved in their kids' endeavors. For example, a mother started to volunteer in an NGO supporting pregnant teens after her daughter learned about teen pregnancy and joined as a volunteer for the NGO; teachers started to meet with peers from their school and other schools on their own time, with teachers overflowing in professional learning sessions (e.g., 900 signed up for sessions originally designed for a couple hundred); and student citizenship was strengthened (explosion of fundraisers created by students to support causes of concern/interest).

In a group of schools, students and teachers decided to study the concept of "beauty" in life, starting with an abstract discussion. Students then explored how to reestablish beauty in the world around them (capturing their own examples of beauty, as well as examples of beauty from their families and friends—domestically and abroad) by fleshing out essential and divergent views of beauty and designing and implementing plans to reestablish beauty in their school and community.

Schools across a district created a role for student "geniuses" serving as technology consultants and trainers to teachers and other adults. A teacher presented a lesson plan, and a student prepared a customized set of tech options to enhance/deepen student learning; young tech experts model and support powerful technology use during Deep Learning professional learning sessions; high school students interviewed and interacted with Grade 1 students (asking for pictures, videos of who they are, what they like) to create narratives capturing who these young people are. More generally, students are opening up teachers' minds to new pedagogies. Teachers and students together are collaborating within and across schools—indeed, across the globe—to discover new ways of learning that are deeply engaging and relevant to their present and future lives and to the future of humanity.

Students, then, are emerging as powerful "change agents" helping to cause the development and circulation of professional capital in a way that no high-profile task force could possibly achieve. Students, deeply involved in meaningful and sophisticated learning projects, represent the most powerful fuel for teachers and administrators, individually and collectively, to radically shift their practice and the conditions that surround it. That is, students as change agents produce substantial shifts in classrooms and in schools and systems (we are currently identifying and classifying examples according to the three categories of pedagogy, learning environment, and society).

> Students are helping to cause the development and circulation of professional capital in a way that no high-profile task force could possibly achieve.

There are several other crucial points to be made about these examples. First, they are the tips of many icebergs. They are occurring more and more frequently. We also see the emergence of parents and families in the equation, but that needs to be the subject of another book. Second, the examples are occurring in everyday schools. Third, they are happening and spreading across schools and systems. The three Ontario districts we studied have 100 or so schools each; they started with a group of about 15 schools each and are now spreading to all of their schools because of value and demand. Fourth, we don't yet see good examples of what I referred to above as

> Students, deeply involved in meaningful and sophisticated learning projects, represent the most powerful fuel for teachers and administrators, individually and collectively, to radically shift their practice and the conditions that surround it.

"organizational change," but take it as a prediction that this will happen: students, educators, and architects will team up to change the physical design of learning environments in ways never before seen.

Fifth, the "helping humanity" theme is a powerful sleeper. Ten-year-olds, for example, do not see helping humanity as a big ask. They take naturally to it as an intrinsic value, not altruistically. With the world in turmoil, students see this kind of citizen-based character as essential for the future of the planet. There are even more radical reasons for the role of the helping humanity theme that I take up in Chapter 6. Sixth, this work is in early formation. Although I believe that Deep Learning will take off rapidly, it requires much focus, discipline, and assessment of impact as it evolves. Seventh, and most fundamentally to this argument, students, as my colleague Peter Senge observes, are less emotionally committed to the status quo and more interested in changing the world *if* they can find a way (P. Senge, personal communication, January 2016). Students are the hidden change agents for changing the profession and the world of learning.

> Students, including very young ones, are becoming citizens of tomorrow today.

What this amounts to is that students, including very young ones, are becoming citizens of tomorrow today. At the same time, their new day-to-day learning is serving a powerful natural "guidance counselor" function unmatched by the most skilled career counselors in our schools. We are seeing this phenomenon time and time again. Students in Grades 4, 5, and 6, for example, are discovering their interests and what they might want to do in life. Most will change their minds and have other ideas, but they are immersed at very young ages in what they might want to do in the future. This early realistic thinking is crucial when we link it to the fact that jobs in the future will not only be radically different but also considerably fewer in number. Deep Learning is real-life learning, exactly at the time that real life is dramatically changing in unknown ways.

We see other powerful examples of students doing amazing things that increase their future life chances, as well as having the potential (if positioned in the way that I am talking about) to change the world toward greater humanity. Tony Wagner and Ted Dintersmith (2015), in their manifesto *Most Likely to Succeed: Preparing Our Kids for the Innovation Era,* furnish countless examples of what the new work looks like and who is doing it, regrettably *despite* the current system. Marc Prensky (2016), in his *Education to Better the World,* provides chapter and verse how kids want to and are improving the world from the ground up. Kids are rockets, he says, and educators need to be rocket scientists. Wagner, Dintersmith, and Prensky base their work, as we do, on ever-increasing numbers of grounded examples, but it won't be enough. We need strategies to make this trend a movement of unstoppable proportions.

Educators must unleash and mobilize their professional capital as a circulating force for individual and societal change. Our best chance of accomplishing this revolution is to get students to help drive the development and flow of professional capital throughout the system.

THE SYMBIOTIC RELATIONSHIP BETWEEN STUDENTS AS CHANGE AGENTS AND THE FUTURE OF THE TEACHING PROFESSION

At the beginning of the chapter, I discussed several large-scale efforts that were designed to transform the profession only to be followed by further deterioration. At some point, you have to wonder whether this direct policy-driven strategy may be the wrong way to go about it (reminding us of Einstein's definition of insanity: doing the same thing over and over again and expecting different results or, if you prefer, redoubling your efforts after you have forgotten your aim). Even the most enlightened policy solutions are bound to fail. For example, Mehta et al.'s (2016) "quicksand to solid ground" remedy barely mentions students, and it basically goes on to the seemingly reasonable but misplaced conclusion that finding better teachers and having them work together will save students.

I identify a different pathway: We need students to save students, liberated by enabling teachers and administrators (and the latter two groups liberated equally by students as change agents). The solid surround is the professional capital of teachers in which the human, social, and decision capital of teachers develop *in two-way partnerships with students and families*. It is only educators, with the increased velocity of circulating professional capital, who will have the wherewithal to be proactive two-way learners with students and families in transforming learning, thereby transforming the teaching profession. Educators will never be able to do this without the proactive agency of students.

We see in this chapter fertile seeds of transformational growth. But we need more. The next stop is to feed and be fed by the system—one more step toward establishing Deep Learning through deep leadership.

> We need students to save students, liberated by enabling teachers and administrators (and the latter two groups liberated equally by students as change agents).

● ● ● ● ACTION STEPS

1. Do you believe students are and can be agents of change? Uncover, discover, be open to, and cultivate the ways in which students can be forces for pedagogical, organizational, and societal change, thereby helping you, helping themselves, and indeed helping humanity.

2. What strategies and practices do you have in place to develop, manage, and maximize the influence of individual talent in your organization? What are the ways in which you could further develop human capital?

3. How strong is the "collective efficacy" in impacting improved practice and results in your culture?

4. What do the people in your organization do on a regular basis to deepen their professional judgment and expertise? What are two short-term and two long-term actions you could take to further develop decision capital in your organization?

CHAPTER
5

Feed and Be Fed by the System

We know that top-down change doesn't work, nor does bottom-up change spread beyond a few isolated places. Our indelible leaders leave a mark on the *system!* How could they possibly do this? The answer is beginning to emerge, and it takes the form of acting as system players, leadership from the middle (that I define shortly), and leading deep change. As we activate the middle and the bottom, we are discovering a fundamental key to changing the status quo. People at the levels below the top may be stuck with the policies of system leaders, but *they are not stuck with their mindsets!* Feeding the system is a matter of mobilizing new mindsets, and when they reach a certain scale, *policies will change.* Feed the system in order to make it better, and then be fed by it.

> People at the levels below the top may be stuck with the policies of system leaders, but *they are not stuck with their mindsets!*

SYSTEM PLAYERS

One of our powerful new concepts that many leaders are attracted to is *systemness*. Systemness occurs when individuals go about their work, making their own best contribution while realizing that they are part of a bigger enterprise that they should contribute to and learn from. On a small scale, for example, when a school moves from an individualistic to a collaborative culture, the following phenomenon happens every time: Teachers stop thinking only of "my kids in my classroom" and start thinking of all students in the school. This is an increment in systemness. Similarly, when principals participate in active networks of schools, they soon become almost as committed to the success of other schools in the network as their own. And when districts work in consortia, as we will see below, the commitment to each other rises.

At the same time, a powerful epiphenomenon is becoming evident. Most humans welcome the idea of making a larger contribution. "System playing" provides a concrete, practical outlet for making a large contribution to society. Such a contribution, because it is practical and big, has an enormous, intrinsic motivational appeal to leaders who want to make a difference. Sure, there is a bit of ego in this, but mostly it is a basic human value to want to make a larger, identifiable contribution to society. Such a possibility is especially appealing to leaders in the educational system because it is so "broken," especially in the United States. The trouble is that for the past thirty years, it has proven impossible in education to make much of a difference. The result has been burnt-out leaders who tried but failed, leaders who enter for the wrong reasons (serial superintendents who make their way and fortune by going from one district to another, leaving a bad taste but not much else), and scores of good people who refuse leadership positions because they know that such moves represent a recipe for frustration and grief, and they have no interest in trying to get better at a bad game.

In short, in terms of the theme of this book, we will not find indelible leaders until we find an angle through which large numbers of leaders find that they can make a difference—a deep difference—in the lives of the adults and students with whom they work.

Systemness is the arena that represents the potential for attracting committed leaders in numbers who could transform the system because they will understand the current system and know it should be changed. They will respect and reject the status quo. So we need strategies that enable systemness to flourish. The next two sections identify two such strategic domains.

LEADERSHIP FROM THE MIDDLE

The logic of leadership from the middle (LftM) starts with the conclusion that neither top-down nor bottom-up change works, and it asks the question, "Where is the glue?" for possible system coherence. We find the glue in the middle. In education, at the state level are the districts, municipalities, and networks of schools lodged in between the top (government) and local schools and communities (one can also shift the identification of the middle by moving to other levels of focus, e.g., for districts/municipalities, the middle is the schools; for schools, the middle is the teachers).

Andy Hargreaves and his colleagues first identified the power of the middle as a force for change and coherence in their study of ten districts in Ontario charged with working together to improve special education and overall literacy (see Hargreaves & Ainscow, 2015, for his latest formulation). Over the past three years, LftM has become the best and most promising hope we have for system transformation. I start by defining it and then provide examples of its growth and presence in big systems with which we work.

> Over the past three years, LftM has become the best and most promising hope we have for system transformation.

The formal definition of LftM for me is *A deliberate strategy that increases the capacity and internal coherence in the middle as it becomes a more effective partner upward to the state and downward to its schools and communities* (Fullan, 2015a, p. 24). We see this movement in New Zealand, where its 2,500 autonomous schools have begun to work in networks (called "community of schools") of from 5 to 15 schools. The purpose is to develop and share focused innovations that increase the efficacy of educators, students, and families to improve the learning of all students within the network, and ultimately across the country (see Fullan, 2015a; New Zealand Ministry of Education, 2015).

Similarly, there is a massive movement in California (that I will describe in a moment) among its 1,009 school districts and 58 counties to establish consortia of districts working collectively to solve specific problems. In Ontario there are several examples of LftM, one of which I will take up in the next section. England also has had more than a decade of academies and federations in which clusters of schools (typically 5–15 schools) gain independent status to focus on school improvement within the network, although the overall strategy lacks focus and commitment to system change.

As we shall see in the following paragraphs, LftM is, indeed, receiving an increasing amount of attention and action. Steve Munby (former head of the National College of School Leadership in England) and I recently established a Global Dialogue webinar on the matter of networks in a paper called "Inside-Out and Downside-Up: How Leading From the Middle Has the Power to Transform Education Systems" (Munby & Fullan, 2016).

In LftM, by design and experiences several interrelated forces become synergized: collaboration and coherence occurs intra-school and intra-district; mutual learning and problem solving occurs inter-district or inter-network; and powerfully, partnership and engagement operates upward to the state. The latter is interesting. In some cases, the center begins to appreciate the power of the middle and invests in it (although we say that we don't want the state to run the initiative, we want them to like it). In other cases, the middle blunts ill-conceived policies. In still others, the middle and center partner to co-develop new polices and strategies for the future.

LftM is so recent that we should be careful not to overclaim. Networks of schools helping each other are not new, but what is different recently is the sheer scale and intentionality of clusters of schools as part and parcel of system change. LftM is almost instantly attractive to good leaders in the middle, and it is generating huge energy, commitment, and action on concrete matters of high importance. The work has several virtues. As Hargreaves and Ainscow (2015) note, LftM stimulates leaders and the group to:

- Respond to local needs and diversities.
- Take collective responsibility for all students, and for each other's success.
- Exercise initiative rather than implementing other people's initiatives.
- Integrate its own efforts with broad system priorities.
- Establish transparency of practice and results. (p. 44)

One place to watch with respect to LftM is California. Larger in population than Canada, California has more than 6 million students, some 1,000 districts, and 58 counties. In the 1980s, California was a leading, innovative state in the country, but it has steadily declined to become one of the lowest-performing states. How would one reverse such a trend? Certainly not by direct top-down leadership, nor by expecting the 1,000 districts to improve on their own.

Our team is working with all levels of the system in California on the very problem of whole-system reform. It is the case that certain developments at the center by Governor Jerry Brown, State Superintendent Tom Torlakson, and the State Board are opening the door by promoting capacity over compliance and decentralization of resources and authority. The center has also reached out with a new sense of partnership, such as the State Superintendent's Task Force on Accountability and Continuous Improvement that is co-chaired by the president of the California Teachers' Association (the largest teachers' union, with 325,000 members), Eric Heins, and the executive director of the Association of California School Administrators, Wes Smith. There is also a parallel partnership with the State Board designed to integrate and produce a new state-level accountability system that is less punitive and more incentive-driven for system improvement.

The Task Force, State Board, and other initiatives represent favorable actions that help set a new direction, but they do not ensure implementation. Only LftM has any chance of mobilizing enough leadership to result in breakthroughs on a large scale. I can only provide a few of the most prominent examples in this space (for an overview of California reform policies and direction, see my three short reports under the banner of *California's Golden Opportunity* at www.michaelfullan.ca). Here are three powerful LftM examples in California, two of which are brand-new.

1. CORE (California Office to Reform Education) is the oldest consortium, founded in 2011 and consisting of nine school districts (including most of the large districts in the state). Its main initial success was political, involving obtaining a federal waiver from No Child Left Behind requirements, but it has also had a capacity-building role for its member districts. In some ways, it is too large and multifaceted to assess its impact, but it certainly legitimized the possibility of LftM leadership. We are working with the CORE districts, with several large pockets of LftM initiatives under way within and across the districts.

2. The more revealing examples of the strategy are brand-new, large, and specific in agenda. A small, catalytic nonprofit entity called California Ed Partners (CAED) has been supporting networks over the past few years and has now sharpened the strategy with new initiatives based explicitly on LftM principles and design. In January 2016, CAED launched a "portfolio" of district collaboratives called CALLI (California Learning and Language Innovation) involving five to six districts working together, totaling at present thirty districts spread over the whole state. The response, willingness, and commitment on the part of districts to collaborate have been spontaneous, with the organizers (CAED) being careful to go slowly in initial setup so that the decision to join would be carefully considered by both CAED and the individual and subgroups of districts. The work of CALLI is designed and supported for learning and implementation and will be carefully evaluated. The work is specific, focusing on the improvement of second-language learning with paired sets of districts zeroing in on particular challenges: two groups of districts are working on early literacy, two on academic

language development, and one set on improving high school mathematics.

3. The third example comes from ACSA, the administrators' association that established its own LftM initiative in the fall of 2015 called the System Leadership Collaborative (SLC). SLC involves fourteen districts (seven in the south of the state and seven in the north) to tackle the thorny problem of how to develop the newly required Local Control Accountability Plan (LCAP). LCAP represents the new state requirement for local district plans whereby each district is required to consult its community, identify goals and priorities, and plan for implementation. LCAP got off to a rocky start. In my third *California's Golden Opportunity* report ("LCAP's Theory of Action" at www.michaelfullan.ca) I named the problems: making complexity complicated, overdoing the front-end process, and making the plan itself the goal. The initial result is that the first LCAP plans ranged from 57 pages to 450! Nobody intended this degree of bureaucracy, but old habits die hard. In SLC, the fourteen districts are working to focus LCAP on targeted strategies for improvement.

The SLC is intended to use the knowledge and skills of the middle to further local implementation and to improve a state policy. The first efforts are encouraging. Barely started, the initial idea and experiences of the SLC was presented to the annual Superintendents' Symposium in January 2016. The reaction from the group was widespread excitement for the prospect of using LCAP to simplify the process and place districts in a leadership role in partnership with each other and other levels of the system. Several of the SLC district superintendents in attendance reported that in eight months, they have significantly changed how they are leading their districts by changing the focus of questions they ask their district leaders with respect to improving practices and support for student learning. We can attest to the substance of the developments within SLC districts as we are part of supporting SLC as it evolves.

Of course, excitement and the desire to work together for fundamental change are not system transformation, but one can readily see how many leaders are coming to the table, how they are working differently, how they are learning from each other, and how the sheer number of connected leaders increases the desire for intra-district development, cross-district learning, and partnerships with the state. At the same time, our team is working with several County Offices of Education (recall there are 58 counties overseeing the 1,000 districts—counties that, among other responsibilities, are charged with approving local district plans in the new decentralized system). The counties as an organization have also officially endorsed capacity building over compliance, but implementation is another matter.

It is this mobilization and concentration of leaders in the middle— districts and counties—that has a chance of developing focus and coherence on a scale large enough to change the performance of the system, even one as large as California. If it goes deep enough, it may have staying power, and if, as we shall see in Chapter 6, leaders develop their teams (leaders developing leaders), it could have carryover power in the future.

For my purposes here, I will oversimplify by saying that our team is involved with the whole state of California, simultaneously working on macro cohesion (state polices and strategies) and micro cohesion (regional, county, and district strategies). Cohesion at the micro level needs to have a degree of freedom from the top (like us but don't run us) as it takes into account local and state policy. Cohesion at the macro level involves general direction, investment in leadership from the middle networks, and what we call a "project and protect" orientation to the system, intervening selectively in the case of persistently poor performance (see Chapter 5 of Fullan & Quinn, 2016, where we examine "securing accountability").

Still, it is not enough. We need, as we saw in the last chapter, to extend leadership so that it activates and responds to unleashed energy at the bottom—students and teachers. For this to happen, we need leadership for deep change, and if this phenomenon does not take hold at the bottom, it ain't deep. I will return to this matter in Chapter 6.

I have focused on practice rather than research in this chapter (although my modus operandi is that all good practice reflects and fuels research). To rein- force our practice-based findings in this chapter, I refer to a review of research on the charac-

> We need to extend leadership so that it activates and responds to unleashed energy at the bottom.

teristics of effective networks that Santiago Rincón-Gallardo and I just published. We found eight essential characteristics of quality networks:

1. Focusing on ambitious student learning outcomes linked to effective pedagogy;

2. Developing strong relationships of trust and internal accountability;

3. Continuously improving practice and systems through cycles of collaborative inquiry;

4. Using deliberate leadership and skilled facilitation within flat power structures;

5. Frequently interacting and learning inward;

6. Connecting outward to learn from others;

7. Forming new partnership among students, teachers, families, and communities; and

8. Securing adequate resources to sustain the work. (Rincón-Gallardo & Fullan, 2016, p. 10)

LftM examples in this chapter reflect these characteristics, as we have seen, but all of these efforts need to be carefully evaluated in terms of impact and lessons being learned. My point is that LftM is arriving on the scene in a big way and with focus. Although LftM is a major force, it will not be sufficient. It can, as we have seen, affect the middle and can have influence upward. To use the title of the chapter, such leaders are feeding the system, and the more that they do this the more bountiful the system becomes as a feeding ground for all leaders. I also caution the reader that LftM cannot be seen as the latest "bullet." Any given example of LftM has to be carried out with precision, depth, and commitment to impact. Above all, it must be part and parcel of the agenda I have articulated across all of the chapters in this book—mobilizing all levels of the system for deep change.

Despite my obvious optimism reflected in this book and this chapter, change forces still favor the status quo. To address this stuck state will require new persistent leadership within and across all three levels (top, middle, and bottom) but especially from the bottom upward (the bottom is less invested in the status quo) and the middle inward, upward, and downward. This is why I have cast students as radical change agents in the previous chapter and why the middle needs to see itself as a force for up and down change. Think of it this way: For more than forty years we have known the characteristics of effective collaborative schools and the benefits they bring to teachers and students alike (Fullan, 2015b). Yet the number of such schools has barely moved beyond a ceiling of a third or so. The biggest problem still persists, namely, that the "variation of performance" within schools is greater than the variation between schools, but both types of variation need to be tackled (Hattie, 2015). Good collaboration, as we say, reduces bad variation (ineffective practice) and increases good variation (innovations that deepen learning). Currently the legacy culture adversely affects both kinds of variation, failing to address ineffective practice while inhibiting the circulation of new ideas.

In short, we need to reduce ineffective variation as we increase access to better ideas within and between schools. To do this, we need to mobilize new learning that steps outside the confined cultures of the past. School people need to "go outward in order to look inward," thereby examining what they are doing in light of what others are doing, as well as contributing to others. Going outside contributes to others, but more important, it is the way to improve one's own situation. You go outside in order to get better inside.

> You go outside in order to get better inside.

Although the power of collaborative cultures has been known for several decades, as I said above, it has recently been formulated with a sharper edge. Hargreaves and I (2012) did this with our concept of *Professional Capital*. Hattie (2015) has now declared *collective efficacy* as the queen of effect sizes on student learning. In business, Leinwand and Mainardi (2016) found that all successful companies that they studied—companies that were masters at reducing the "strategy-to-execution gap"—had three facets of culture in common: "emotional commitment, mutual accountability, and collective mastery" (p. 121). In our work we are also helping to mobilize students and families as change agents.

The leadership required to create such cultures of collective efficacy is currently at a premium and represents another reason why we need people to challenge the existing state of affairs as they develop other leaders who can do the same. Given the depth of problems, and given what we know about the direction and nature of the solution as depicted in this book, it is time to be bold!

Looking upward, the change principle emerging here is that in whatever level of the system you reside, you should want the level above you to like what you are doing but not control it—student to teacher, teacher to principal, principal to district, district to state.

Looking downward, you need to enable the work of the next level down, invest in LftM, and establish the conditions of effective accountability (i.e., transparency and precision of practice, evidence-based results, a developmental mindset, and selective intervention).

The revolutionary idea in this book is that the bottom feeders are actually not bottom feeders. They should no longer be seen and treated as those picking up the scraps of whatever the hierarchy serves up. Rather, they are the source of transformation. Lasting change is deep change, and it will not happen if students and

> In whatever level of the system you reside, you should want the level above you to like what you are doing but not control it—student to teacher, teacher to principal, principal to district, district to state.

teachers are not active agents in this enterprise. We saw in Chapter 4 that students have huge potential, not only to serve themselves but to serve the organization and society. Students are untapped sources of system transformation for three major interrelated reasons. First, being young, and being peripheral members of schools (the boredom factor), they are the least attached to the status quo. Second, being frustrated by traditional schooling, they emotionally feel the gap between what is and what could be (even if they don't envisage the latter). Third, as we have seen in Chapter 4, once activated, they intuitively see new possibilities for the future. In short, students are potential forces for transformation en masse.

> It may be that this particular generation of students, at this particular time in history, are primed to help humanity and potentially have access to knowledge, each other, and proactive educators to put a big dent in the status quo.

It may be that this particular generation of students, at this particular time in history, are primed to help humanity and potentially have access to knowledge, each other, and proactive educators to put a big dent in the status quo. They represent leadership from the bottom, analogous to LftM; that is, they need to connect laterally, and they need to connect upward to the next levels. For this movement, and that is exactly what it could be, *a social movement of grand proportions,* they need help, and that help is leadership from other levels: teachers, principals, district, and so on. We have, then, the seeds of indelible leadership.

> Lasting change is deep change, and it will not happen if students and teachers are not active agents in this enterprise.

In summary, the complete story for our purposes is threefold. First, the middle needs to show greater initiative connecting sideways, upward and downward. Second, if the center can recognize the value of the middle it can stimulate, respond to, and otherwise leverage the middle to act and can even appreciate that a strong middle does not comply with policy but critically engages with it.

Third, a similar dynamic occurs at the bottom with a lot more transformational potential. Students can be the most powerful change agents of the lot. Effective leaders wherever they are located pay close attention to all three levels.

The bottom line is that we must go deep with students to have any chance of establishing a new order—one that is tantalizingly showing signs of life but is also ill defined and precarious. I believe that radical change is imminent but also unpredictable—that is why we need indelible leadership that always leaves them learning.

● ● ● ● ACTION STEPS

1. Do you connect laterally with other schools within your district/ region? How could you do this in order to increase the effectiveness of your organization?

2. How can you foster the mindset in your organization that "we may be stuck with external policies, but we are not stuck with mindsets of policy makers"? What strategies can we use so that those at the next level up can like but not "run" what we are doing?

3. Name specific things you could do to "liberate" or give more freedom to those immediately below you in the organizational hierarchy. To be overly dramatic, how can you unleash and partner with the "dogs of system change"—teachers and students?

4. Identify two or three actions you could take to be more of a "system player," contributing to the betterment of the larger entity while benefiting from it.

CHAPTER

6

Be Essential and Dispensable

We will need two major integrated forces to achieve indelible change in education: one involves the relentless focus on Deep Learning—the kind that I described as the six global competencies and their associated pedagogies. The second surge of energy required is *leaders developing other leaders* who focus on the work and on each other. I have tried to provide the ideas, conceptual tools, and strategies that will be essential for cultivating and strengthening the two forces. Leaders are essential to establishing the conditions for deep learning, but they also must have an eye to what will happen after they leave. The skill set for this type of indelible leadership is sixfold—to be employed simultaneously, not sequentially.

> Embody a relentless moral imperative and related uplifting leadership with those you work with.

First, make sure that you embody a relentless moral imperative and related uplifting leadership with those you work with. What you are ultimately doing is promoting in yourself and others the passion and connectedness to take on the Deep Learning agenda. What you will be doing becomes a large part of who you are and why you are on this earth (for your own good and that of others).

> You will need to master both content and process.

Second, you will need to master both content and process. On the one hand, you will have to contend with shaping and reshaping ideas that are important to the journey that you and others undertake; on the other hand, you will need to process the thoughts and actions of others, including their capacity and commitment to what is emerging. This dynamic duo of content and process produces greater individual and collective coherence, which is a *subjective phenomenon*. Recall my definition of coherence as "the shared depth of understanding of the nature of the work." If you master content and process together, you will get greater coherence that will have some staying power, but coherence making always needs to be attended to because people are coming and going, society changes, and new ideas are discovered inside and outside the group. You are indeed always learning, but there is a settling frame to the work because the full set of skills operates to mediate innovation and consolidation—what sets out as a trek becomes a focused journey.

> The balance between leading and learning is essential.

Third, obviously the balance between leading and learning is essential. The moment you get out of balance and don't achieve "equal measure," you get into trouble. Too much leading fails to recognize what might be new and what is going through the minds of others. You get out of touch with the hearts and souls of the group and what excites and perplexes them. Too much learning is a recipe for confusion. At key points, the group needs leaders who can articulate and help test what is being learned. When lots is going on, and when excitement of the new reaches giddy heights, people need help to focus. Leading and learning means that sometimes it is necessary to not fully know what you are doing (or you will never explore the unknown), while other times you need to take stock and

> See students as change agents.

draw some conclusions. Equal measure leaders calibrate the push and pull dynamic of leading and learning.

Fourth, I suggested that discovering students as change agents is the surest way to generate powerful pedagogy. Teachers need to develop and integrate their human, social, and decision capital, both individually and collectively. I argued that the secret ingredient for doing this is none other than the students who are right under our noses. Strange as it may sound at first, the new building block of transformation involves unleashing the role of students as change agents to radically alter (a) the pedagogy of teachers (toward co-learning partnerships with students); (b) the way the school and its environment are organized for learning; and (c) how society evolves toward a helping humanity set of skills and commitment that excites and engages young and old alike in improving the world through local and global action. Student as deep learners are both protégés requiring mentors and change agents for their teachers. Students, too, learn and lead.

Fifth, all of this accelerates when leaders use deliberate strategies to become and help others become "system players"—when people cycle in and out of their own bailiwick and become engaged laterally and vertically. It is this sideways and up and down expansion of purposeful learning that builds a system that is being fed by its leaders, as it reciprocates by feeding the system as a whole.

Sixth, the job description of the indelible leader is to develop collaborative cultures (of the type that I have been portraying) for five or more years, to the point where you become *dispensable* to your group—a blow to the ego in the smaller scheme of things but a grand contribution for indelible leadership. Deep leaders should think of themselves as being essential for the present and, in a real sense, critical to the future. Every leader leaves at some point, and if too much depends on you, the chances for continuity are seriously compromised. If, on the other hand, you develop leaders upon leaders along the lines of the previous five chapters, you have greatly increased the chances that you will, in effect, keep on giving long after you are gone (and you don't have to be *gone* gone; you can go on to bigger and better things).

> Develop collaborative cultures for five or more years, to the point where you become *dispensable* to your group—a blow to the ego in the smaller scheme of things but a grand contribution for indelible leadership.

What is happening is that you have helped develop many leaders in the short run who can go deeper and wider. Together you accomplish things that have never before been possible. But more than that, the junior members of the team, so to speak, become the next generation of leaders for the future as they, too, have the capacity to go even deeper and to develop other leaders who can do the same, and so on. Leaders developing leaders, with focus and depth, is your legacy (if you want to be self-centered), and it is how the world gets better (if we want humankind to survive).

I have not addressed in this book *how* leaders can become adept at managing the six sets of tensions. I can't take this up in detail, but I can identify a powerful line of development for the would-be "indelible leader." Anders Ericsson, the researcher Malcolm Gladwell made famous by citing the 10,000-hour rule that states that anybody can be an expert if they put in 10,000 hours of practice, has just written a book with Robert Pool, *Peak*, to set the record straight (2016). It turns out that what makes the difference is *cumulative deliberative practice.*

Long a tenet of our approach, this is the idea that you have to get better through doing the work itself with a "purposeful practice mindset." Ericsson says that purposeful practice has four characteristics: (1) it has well-defined, specific goals, (2) it is focused, (3) it involves feedback, and (4) it requires getting out of one's comfort zone (Ericsson & Pool, 2016, pp. 15–17). It is true that the skill and knowledge base is better codified in the performance arts (music, sports, chess), but he provides many examples from less determined disciplines like teaching. For leadership, he says, "our starting point is the measurement of performance in the real world" (personal communication, April 2016).

Indelible leadership—managing the six sets of tensions—is hard to document, let alone assess for impact. But we have some starting points. In every case of expert performance, leaders in their field become much better at what Ericsson calls "mental representations" of the situation at hand, which he defines as "a mental structure that corresponds to an object, an idea, a collection of information, or anything else, concrete or abstract, that the brain is thinking about" (Ericsson & Pool, 2016, p. 58). The good news is that almost all of us can get better over time at almost anything (physical attributes notwithstanding) through deliberate practice. As Ericsson puts it:

> The main thing that sets experts apart from the rest of us is that their years of experience have changed the neural circuitry in the brain to produce highly specialized mental representations, which in turn make possible the incredible memory, pattern recognition, problem solving, and other sorts of advanced abilities needed to excel in their particular specialties. (p. 63)

We see this in our favorite sports heroes: they can see the bigger picture, anticipate the next moves, identify patterns without thinking about them, and so on. Experts—and we can imagine this in leaders who can manage the six tensions—are better at deciphering complex situations. In anticipating reactions or future developments, experts have the "ability to envision more possible outcomes and quickly sift through them and come up with the most promising action" (p. 64).

We have a long way to go in education to improve teaching, leadership, and other domains. The sad part is that professionals get better in their first few years of experience and then stagnate. Additional years of experience and no amount of traditional professional development make much of a difference in improving performance. It is only job-embedded practice over time, with a coach, a mentor, and critical, specific feedback, that increases the ability to handle complex situations. Neither greater knowledge, nor more experience per se, helps very much. It is skill relative to the problem at hand that makes the difference.

Ericsson's analyses open up a whole new agenda for developing educators which, I believe, will become part of future landscape of transforming preparation and learning on the job. For now, the reader would be well advised to examine the six tensions, identify role models, mentors, and coaches who can help them, engage in deliberate practice relative to the tensions, be alert to impact (what works and doesn't work), and look for progress in how you can recognize problems with greater perspective (mental representations at work). The tensions themselves form a curriculum for leadership development. Those who become accomplished have a special responsibility relative to the sixth tension: be essential to the continuous cultivation of a new generation of deep leaders.

There is an additional crucial reason why leaders these days must foster leadership in others—namely, that the turnover rate for leaders is especially high. Due mostly to demographics and instability in the labor market, a high percentage of leaders are leaving; in many situations, up to a third or more are departing over a three- or four-year period and need to be replaced.

> Deep learning produces graduates who are exquisitely suited to the future.

Formal and informal mentoring on the job plays a dual role. It produces more leaders for the tasks at hand, and it paves the way for a future generation of leaders. Lead them learning today so that you can leave them learning for tomorrow. Replenishing leadership is and always will be a continuous requirement.

We recently received from the business sector fundamental confirmation of the themes that I have been discussing in this book. LRN's *HOW Report* examined governance, culture, and leadership as they impacted performance. In a study involving 16,000 employees in 17 countries, LRN documented that organizations that had "self-governance cultures" outperformed other companies by a long shot (LRN, 2016). The definition and measure of such cultures consisted of

> purpose-inspired, values-based organizations that are led with moral authority and operate with a set of core principles and social imperatives. Employees are inspired by a desire for significance and encouraged to act as leaders regardless of role. Such organizations are focused on long-term legacy and sustainable performance. (LRN, 2016, p. 5)

LRN also found that "managers who emphasize shaping character and fostering freedom are more effective leaders" and that "the key enabler of innovation is trust" (p. 10). Taking risks, celebrating, collaborating, sharing information, and speaking out behaviors were all more evident in the effective organizations (defined as generating greater engagement and productivity). In other words, the nature of deep leadership described in previous chapters, and the new pedagogies that focus on the 6Cs—the global competencies— produce graduates who are exquisitely suited to the high- performing organizations of the future! Deep learning school sys- tems are fundamentally on the right track. Education leaders must lead them learning, and leave them learning—something that graduates will take forward for the rest of their lives. The critical importance of investing in the leadership of young members of the organization is something that was confirmed in the recent global Deloitte survey of 7,700 millennials (born in the 1982–2000 period). Supporting leadership development was the strongest fac- tor that built loyalty to the organization.

I said in the Preface that the education system, especially in the United States, is in a dangerously sorry state. My next point was not that the condition was so sorry that it is bound to improve, but that there were new forces appearing that had great appeal and power to transform the system. I am willing to think that this may be social evolution at work, but no matter. Deep work, leadership therein, leadership from the middle, and students as agents of change represent a powerful concoction—powerful enough *to cause* system transformation because it attracts in geometrically expanding order a critical mass of forces at all levels of the system to do the work of change and consolidation.

There is a radical need to prepare differently for the future: to enable "helping humanity" to become our strength. We are getting the sense that new forces will combine to make the future either radically threatening or excitingly better for humankind. Proliferation of robots, concentration of wealth, and unchecked climate change could combine to spell disaster. Or we could handle them differently, as Douglas Rushkoff (2016) entertains:

> If we are measuring our health in terms of growth, then we are on the wrong track. If we are depending more on our competence, getting closer to value creation, allowing others to participate, investing in bounded communities where we actually live, and operating businesses we want to sustain instead of sell, then chances are we are moving in the right direction: grounded, collaborative, person-to-person exchange and support. (p. 239)

Robots, and some version of distributed resources, could give us more time to be human. Being human means more time to do things that are intrinsically engaging—to create and make things that have value, to look after others, to pursue personal interests, and so on. The deep learning and deep leadership that I have outlined in this book is both a means of heading toward this state and a means of flourishing once you get there. If we start producing students en masse as "humanity helpers"—and we know there is a huge appetite within children and youth to want this for themselves and for others—it will be our best bet for covering the present as we shape an otherwise dangerous future.

> If we start producing students en masse as "humanity helpers," it will be our best bet for covering the present as we shape an otherwise dangerous future.

All of this is tremendously exciting and stupefying. And it is grist for the mill for the deep leader. You are needed more than ever. We can now identify the components of Deep Learning, but we do not know how they will turn out, each in its own right, let alone their interactive effects. We also know that there are new, prodigious, and unpredictable forces at work that we have never before experienced, and we cannot predict how they will turn out. Transformation needs a kick start. We are finding that the first step in deep learning consists of a combination of awe and doubt followed by the unleashing of energy and excitement. Deep leadership is crucial at this early stage in order to give confidence and support for people to enter the messiness of the new as their natural tendencies to explore and exploit the unknown unfold. In short, deep leadership is crucial at this particular moment in history.

It is time for deep leadership to step to the plate. Leave a mark—a deep, durable mark if you can—to deepen the learning agenda today, while you help other people learn how to learn and to lead on this very agenda. Start a cycle: Always leave them learning so that they, in turn, can always leave others learning! Know

> Start a cycle: Always leave them learning so that they, in turn, can always leave others learning!

that there will be no ordinary future—be prepared to face the unknown with as many learning weapons as you can muster.

● ● ● ● ACTION STEPS

1. If you were to leave your organization today, would it be able to sustain and surpass the work you've led so far? What resources and capacities do you need to have in place to ensure greater sustainability of your organization's improvement work?

2. Review the Action Steps at the end of Chapters 1–5. What practices could you incorporate into your everyday work to increase the likelihood of greater impact on student learning in the long run?

3. Legacy pedagogy and legacy culture favor the status quo. What bold or innovative steps could you take to promote Deep Learning in your organization? Push the envelope.

4. Be worried and fascinated by the future. Find ways you can leverage humanity.

References

Bryant, A. (2013, November 2). Honeywell's David Cote, on decisiveness as a 2-edged sword. *New York Times.* Retrieved from http://www.nytimes.com.

Campbell, C., Lieberman, A. & Yashkina, A. (2015). Teachers leading educational improvements: Developing teachers' leadership, improving practices, and collaborating to share knowledge. *Leading & Managing, 21*(2), 90–105.

Carnegie Forum on Education and the Economy. (1986). *A nation prepared: Teachers for a 21st century.* New York, NY: Author.

Carnegie Foundation. (2001). *Teachers for a new era.* New York, NY: Author.

Deloitte. (2016). *The 2016 Deloitte millennial survey: Winning over the next generation of leaders.* Retrieved from www.deloitte.com/millennial survey.html.

Dixon, B. (2016). *The end of school as we know it.* Bloomington, IN: Solution Tree.

Ericsson, A., &, Pool, R. (2016). *Peak: Secrets from the new science of expertise.* New York, NY: Houghton Mifflin.

Fullan, M. (2013). *Stratosphere: Integrating technology, pedagogy, and change knowledge.* Toronto, ON: Pearson.

Fullan, M. (2014). *The principal: Three keys to maximizing impact.* San Francisco, CA: Jossey-Bass.

Fullan, M. (2015a, December). Leadership from the middle. *Education Canada, 55*(4).

Fullan, M. (2015b). *The new meaning of educational change* (5th ed.). New York, NY: Teachers College Press.

Fullan, M. (2015c, December 14). Why helping humanity should be core to learning. *NationSwell.* Retrieved from http://nationswell.com/students-help-humanity-core-learning.

Fullan, M., & Quinn, J. (2016). *Coherence: The right drivers in action for schools, districts, and systems.* Thousand Oaks, CA: Corwin.

Goffee, R., & Jones, G. (2015). *Why should anyone work here?* Boston, MA: Harvard Business Review Press.

Hargreaves, A., & Ainscow, M. (2015, November). The top and bottom of leadership and change. *Phi Delta Kappan, 97*(3), 42–48.

Hargreaves, A., Boyle, A., & Harris, A. (2014). *Uplifting leadership: How organizations, teams, and communities raise performance.* San Francisco, CA: Jossey-Bass.

Hargreaves, A., & Fullan, M. (2012). *Professional capital: Transforming teaching in every school.* New York, NY: Teachers College Press.

Hattie, J. (2012). *Visible learning for teachers.* New York, NY: Routledge.

Hattie, J. (2015). *What works best in education: The politics of collaborative expertise.* London, UK: Pearson.

Kaufman, S. D., & Gregoire, C. (2015). *Wired to create: Unraveling the mysteries of the creative mind.* New York, NY: Penguin Random House.

Leinwand, P., & Mainardi, C. (2016). *Strategy: How winning companies close the strategy to execution gap.* Boston, MA: Harvard Business Review Press.

LRN. (2016). *The HOW Report: A global empirical analysis of how governance, culture, and leadership impact performance.* Retrieved from www.LRN.com.

Martin, R., & Osberg, S. (2015). *Getting beyond better: How social entrepreneurship works.* Boston, MA: Harvard Business Review Press.

Mehta, J. (2013). *The allure of order: High hopes, dashed expectations, and the troubled quest to remake American schooling.* New York, NY: Oxford University Press.

Mehta, J., & Fine, S. (2015). *The why, what, where, and how of deeper learning in American secondary schools.* Boston, MA: Jobs for the Future.

Mehta, J., Theisin-Homer, V., Braslow, D., & Lopatin, A. (2015). *From quicksand to solid ground: Building a foundation to support quality teaching.* Cambridge, MA: Transforming Teaching.

Munby, S., & Fullan, M. (2016). *Inside out and downside–up: How leadership from the middle has the power to transform education systems.* London, UK: Education Development Trust.

National Commission on Excellence in Education. (1983). *A nation at risk.* Washington, DC: Author.

National Commission on Teaching and America's Future. (1996). *What matters most: Teaching for America's future.* Washington, DC: Author.

New Pedagogies for Deep Learning. (2016). Retrieved from http://www.npdl.global.

Newport, C. (2012). *So good they can't ignore you: Why skills trump passion in the quest for work you love.* New York, NY: Business Plus.

Newport, C. (2016). *Deep work: Rules for focused success in a distracted world.* New York, NY: Grand Central.

New Zealand Ministry of Education. (2015). *IES communities of schools guide for schools and Kura.* Wellington, NZ: Author.

Pink, D. (2009). *Drive: The surprising truth about what motivates us.* New York, NY: Riverhead Books.

Prensky, M. (2016). *Education to better their world.* New York, NY: Teachers College Press.

Rincón-Gallardo, S., & Fullan, M. (2016). Essential features of effective collaboration. *Journal of Professional Capital and Community, 1*(1), 5–22.

Robinson, V. (2011). *Student-centered leadership.* San Francisco, CA: Jossey-Bass.

Rushkoff, D. (2016). *Throwing rocks at the Google bus: How growth became the enemy of prosperity.* New York, NY: Penguin.

Wagner, T., & Dintersmith, T. (2015). *Most likely to succeed: Preparing our kids for the innovation era.* New York, NY: Scribner.

Watkins, A. (2014). *Coherence: The secret science of brilliant leadership.* London, UK: Kogan Page.

Index

Acknowledgments

I love my immediate team: Eleanor Adam, Claudia Cuttress, Mary Jean Gallagher, Peter Hill, Bill Hogarth, Terry Jakobsmeier, Joanne Quinn, Joanne McEachen, Santiago Rincón-Gallardo, Joelle Rodway, Nancy Watson; and a special shout-out to Roger Martin for helping to streamline the main framework. Love the scores of Deep Learners in our global partnership.

I love my funders: Stuart Foundation and Hewlett Foundation.

I love my publisher, Corwin, and its people: Mike Soules, Lisa Shaw, Arnis Burvikovs, Melanie Birdsall, Peter DeWitt, Andrew Olson, Diana Breti, and the full team of talented depth at Corwin.

I love my family: Wendy, Conor, Bailey, Josh, Maureen, Chris, spouses, and grandchildren.

What's not to love?

About the Author

Social Imagery

Michael Fullan, Order of Canada, is professor emeritus at the Ontario Institute for Studies in Education, University of Toronto. He served as special adviser in education to former premier of Ontario Dalton McGuinty from 2003 to 2013 and now serves as one of four advisers to Premier Kathleen Wynne. He has been awarded honorary doctorates from the University of Edinburgh, the University of Leicester, Nipissing University, Duquesne University, and the Hong Kong Institute of Education. He consults with governments and school systems in several countries.

Fullan has won numerous awards for his more than thirty books, including the 2015 Grawemeyer Award in Education with Andy Hargreaves for *Professional Capital*. His books include the best sellers *Leading in a Culture of Change*, *The Six Secrets of Change*, *Change Leader*, *All Systems Go*, *Motion Leadership*, and *The Principal: Three Keys to Maximizing Impact*. His latest books are *Evaluating and Assessing Tools in the Digital Swamp* (with Katelyn Donnelly), *Leadership: Key Competencies for Whole-System Change* (with Lyle Kirtman), *The New Meaning of Educational Change* (5th edition), *Freedom to Change*, and *Coherence* (with Joanne Quinn). To learn more, visit his website at www.michaelfullan.ca.

A SAGE Publishing Company

CORWIN HAS ONE MISSION: to enhance education through intentional professional learning.

We build long-term relationships with our authors, educators, clients, and associations who partner with us to develop and continuously improve the best evidence-based practices that establish and support lifelong learning.

ONTARIO
PRINCIPALS'
COUNCIL
Exemplary Leadership in Public Education

The Ontario Principals' Council (OPC) is a voluntary association for principals and vice-principals in Ontario's public school system. We believe that exemplary leadership results in outstanding schools and improved student achievement. To this end, we foster quality leadership through world-class professional services and supports. As an ISO 9001 registered organization, we are committed to **"quality leadership—our principal product."**